*D*oyle *F*amily *C*ounseling *C*enter
"Helping Others Heal Their Hurts"
*****

Testimonials

The following quotes are from people who have been in therapy at *Doyle Family Counseling Center*. The stories in *Change Is A Choice* are about people like those who have written these testimonials.

People Are Talking About
The Doyle Family Counseling Center

"Our family was in deep trouble when we came to DFCC, and the prospects of getting things worked out seemed extremely dim. Little did we know that the warmth, care, and skills of Leanne, Matt, and Don would turn us completely around. How grateful we are to them for saving our family."

Family from Georgia

"After my week with Don, after 60 years, I met myself, the *real me* for the first time. With my uncontrollable temper, I was my own worst enemy; not remotely conscious that I was taking out all of my frustrations on the one person I loved the most—my beautiful wife.

As a result of Don's therapy, we are back together and have committed ourselves to a lifetime of love and understanding on a level we never knew before. Thank you Don, for all you did for us. You are truly incredible."

General Manager, Oregon

"My life and my family were a mess. When my son was in a near-fatal auto accident and left partially paralyzed, it was a final blow, and the last threads began to unravel. Finding Don and Matt Doyle literally saved our lives. With their help, we are putting the pieces back in place and finally beginning to live again. Thank you, Don and Matt...for helping us to recapture our love, our faith, and our joy. We are forever grateful."

Real Estate Agent, Tennessee

"I was in Don's therapy group in Burlingame during the mid-80's. It was a time to be remembered. Since then, I have always kept in touch. I'd always see him for a session when he came back to San Francisco. Then I came to Memphis for an intensive. What a feeling of rejoicing...

I've come a long way baby!"

Woman Entrepreneur, San Francisco

"I laughed, I cried. It was better than Cats!"

California Composer

"I had been depressed all my life. It had affected my work, my family, and my marriage. During my intensive, I discovered that the source of my depression was anger turned inward. The problem was—I have been angry all my life and never done anything with it—except be depressed.

What a relief to unload all that garbage and really start to live. I can't remember feeling such peace. Thanks, Don, for helping me unload my trash!" *Attorney, Michigan*

"For most of my adult life, I have battled depression. I have had therapy before, but this was like no other. Dr. Doyle's approach was so different. It was such a healing experience!

My only regret is that I didn't do this a long time ago. I would heartily recommend to anyone who suffers from depression, anxiety, or hopelessness to get some intensive therapy through DFCC. It will change your life significantly, as it has mine." *Administrative Assistant, Texas*

"Two years ago, I left my husband and moved many states away. I left him over his anger that he found too easy to unload on me. Our lives centered around him and I was just a passenger. He found Don Doyle and the healing process began.

After seeing the change in my husband, I decided to do an intensive, myself. Then we did a week together. It was the best spent time and money we have invested."

Department Store Manager, Oregon

"As a professional who let an important part of my life get away from me, DFCC was a Godsend. The caring and dedication will renew your faith in life."

Appalachian Professional

Professionals Are Talking About
The Doyle Family Counseling Center

"My week at DFCC was an exercise in self-discovery, and was one of the very best weeks of my life. The results greatly exceeded my expectations. I was shocked at how little I knew about myself. I thought my biggest problem was my marriage. I discovered that my biggest problem was ME. I've never experienced such peace. Thanks." *Physician, West Virginia*

"I've worked with several approaches to counseling and several different counselors. Don Doyle's approach and style are the best I've experienced. I've always gotten the most for my money with Don. It's very hard work. But I am convinced that one can gain much more, with longer lasting results, from DFCC's intensive approach than from any other form of therapy." *Pastoral Counselor, North Carolina*

"An intensive session with Don Doyle is a *treat* and a *treatment*. Dr. Doyle has a unique ability to help you do whatever you most need to do! You may talk, sing, cry, laugh, shout, feel intense emotion, or remain reverently quiet. He will help you to heal, grow, and change in a most positive way." *Licensed Counselor, Illinois*

"For persons who have experienced unresolved emotional hurts or trauma in their lives, and who want to heal their traumatic wounds, Dr. Don Doyle is the best therapist available anywhere. My assessment is based on ten years of nationwide research to identify the most effective therapy and most effective therapist to treat PTSD." *Educational Researcher, Illinois*

"Don Doyle helped us create a new vision for our lives. By helping us strip away the pain and confusion from the past, we were able to move beyond and live a life that is exciting and fulfilling.

Not only did we get unstuck, but we learned how to

envision and revision on an ongoing basis so that we are continually growing."

Psychotherapist, California

"Change IS a choice—and fortunately I knew that Dr. Doyle could help with change in our marriage the way he had helped me to personally overcome a devastating miscarriage. I believe that the tools he gave us in our intensive can help ANY marriage get back on track.

Don's wisdom and insights have been nothing short of miraculous at times, but then he depends on the Lord for them. So, if you come, expect miracles."

Educator in Hilo, Hawaii

"Working with Don Doyle reminded me of a cherished ballet teacher who would place me in the proper positions, (which often took quite a bit of pulling, pushing, and lifting on her part), so I could have some idea of where I was trying to go. It was painful, but not injurious, and quite inspiring to see my foot up over my head even though it had taken more than my own strength to get it there. There were aspects of my intensive that were just as austere, yet just as helpful."

Psychiatrist, Texas

"Last year at this time, I was very close to suicide. Now, I'm glad I didn't do it! I would have missed a lot of good stuff. Don Doyle brought me from *soul-sad* to almost glad. He guided me from there to here, but I never saw how or when he did it. Thanks, Don." *Teacher from Tennessee*

"I was a very angry woman...at ex-husband, current lover, former therapist, my son...basically all men. I wasn't keen on working with another male therapist, but the intensive program was intriguing, so I tried it. It changed my life. I finally uncovered and released the hurt that was causing the anger. What a relief."

Entrepreneur, Ohio

GOING SANE
SERIES
Vol. II

****

Change
Is A
Choice

Common People
Who Made
Uncommon Choices

*****

Don Doyle, DMin, PhD

****

Asa HOUSE Books
Memphis, TN 1998

Going Sane
Series
Vol. II

Change is a Choice

by

Don Doyle, DMin, PhD

Illustrations by Roe Kienle

Published by:

Asa HOUSE Books
P.O. Box 381604
Memphis, TN 38183
901/ 751-4140

Copyright @ 1998
First Printing 1998

Library of Congress Catalog Number 98-66695

Doyle, Don
ISBN 1-57087-415-8
170 Pages
$19.95

About the Author

Since 1966, Dr. Don Doyle has functioned in some official capacity as a psychotherapist, minister, or counselor. In that period of time, he has logged more than 35,000 hours of listening to people from forty-two states and eighteen foreign countries.

With degrees in biology (BS), theology (MDiv and DMin), and marriage and family counseling (PhD), Dr. Doyle brings a varied background to the therapy room. In addition, he was in the pastoral ministry for thirteen years, ten of which was spent in one church.

Prior to entering the ministry, he served as a Naval Aviation Officer. As he puts it, "I joined the Navy to see the world and spent three years in Florida. But the value of my military experience was equal to a post-graduate degree."

While serving in the navy, he received special commendation awards from the French, Italian, and Australian navies.

As a popular speaker and lecturer, Dr. Doyle has conducted numerous seminars and conferences, and delivered after-dinner speeches all across the country. He speaks to churches, civic clubs, corporations, and counseling centers. In addition, he has made many guest appearances on radio and television.

For eight years, he was Associate Director of the *Burlingame* (California) *Counseling Center*. Since 1987, he has directed the *Doyle Family Counseling Center* in Memphis, Tennessee.

Married since 1963 to Martha Longmire Doyle, they have three adult children and two grandchildren.

Also by Don Doyle

<u>Heroes of the Heart</u>

Dedicated

To

Matt, Leanne, Chad

From whom I continue to learn about parenthood

****

James Matthew was our first child. He was born in Pensacola, Florida, just a few weeks before Martha and I turned twenty-three. As we were leaving the Navy hospital, the young corpsman who handed him to me made this profound and prophetic statement: "Sir, just remember, he'll bend a lot before he breaks."

Since the firstborn is somewhat like a laboratory rat on whom parents *learn how to parent,* those words became my mantra in parenting Matt. Thank God, the young corpsman was right. Even with all my parental goofups, he certainly did *bend a lot without breaking.*

When Matt was young, he and I frequently sang: "You and me are gonna be partners, you and me are gonna be pals, you and me are gonna be partners-- partners, buddies, and pals." That, too, was prophetic because he still is my partner, buddy, and pal.

Mary Leanne was born in Louisville, Kentucky, almost four years after Matt. Don't know if we learned anything in those prior *parental experimentation years,* but I do know she was delightfully easy to parent. Even as the middle child, she never showed any of the negative traits common to that birthorder.

As the only daughter and sister, she's always had a unique place in our family. And she has managed that position in the most exemplary fashion. She has always been a great friend to all of us, and is a splendid role model in every aspect of her life.

When she was young, she didn't care very much for sleeping. She was afraid she'd miss something. She hasn't changed a lot in that area. Up to this point in her life, I don't think she's missed very much either.

To top it off, Leanne has been and always will be *Daddy's Girl.*

Walter Chad was born in Homerville, Georgia, and joined our family four years after Leanne. As our last child, and the proverbial *baby of the family,* indeed, he has occupied a special place. No doubt, he has benefited from being in that position. Don't know how Chad pulled it off, but Matt and Leanne never treated him like a *little brother who was a brat.* He was always welcomed and included in their activities.

Although Martha and I had not turned thirty-one when he was born, it still felt as if he were the child of our *later years.* One thing is for sure. Chad has been a consistent ray of sunshine in my life.

One thing more. I've always revered, respected, and relished Chad's ability to relate so well to all people. Now that he's a full-fledged young adult, I'm more impressed every day.

To

Matt, Leanne, Chad

With appreciation, admiration, and affection
December 1997

Preface

The GOING SANE SERIES is about people; real people dealing with real problems. It's about people like you and me whose journey to find contentment in life has been sprinkled with some successes and failures.

Of the many blessings in my life, one that I deeply cherish is the privilege I've had in listening to these people share their experiences. As a card-carrying *official listener* since 1966, I've logged more than 35,000 hours of listening to people's stories.

"As long as you've been doing this, I guess you've heard it all," someone periodically says to me.

It's true. Over that many years, a large portion of the problems, circumstances, and stories are quite similar.

"You must get bored to tears hearing the same old stuff, over and over," is also said with some frequency.

However, the amazing thing is that no two stories are exactly alike, thus, never boring. And as surprising as it may seem, with consistent regularity, someone always has a new story unlike anything I've heard before.

Change is a Choice is the second volume in the *Going Sane Series*. Like the first volume, Heroes of the Heart, it's a composite of essays and short stories about some of these experiences and some of these people. It's about *common people who made uncommon choices.*

Some of the stories are inspirational; others are controversial. Some of the pieces will make you sad, mad, or glad. Believing as I do, that humor is one of life's greatest gifts, hopefully you will find some comic relief scattered throughout.

My highest hope is that these stories will provide the motivation and inspiration for you to *choose to change* your life in whatever way YOU choose.

The people in these stories have honored me by sharing their journeys with me. It is my desire to pay tribute to them by sharing these experiences with you.

All the stories are true. All the people are real. However, **the names and the locations are totally fictitious** (except when specified). Any resemblance to anyone you know is purely coincidental.

This book was written as a dialogue with each reader. Therefore, the writing style is strictly conversational.

*****

Throughout these pages, there are several references regarding the therapy programs at DFCC. Such terms as *intensives, aftercare plans, Intensive Relational Integration Therapy, IRIT, reliving and releasing, and follow-up* appear frequently. For details about these terms and our program, see pages 163-170.

Acknowledgments

The acknowledgment page of this book is my feeble effort to express gratitude to those who helped with this project. For me, it is the most difficult page to write in the entire volume. Not difficult because I'm ungrateful; difficult because this seems like an inept method of expressing my true feelings. Nonetheless, since I would be remiss if no attempt were made, here goes.

Special kudos to Roe Kienle for another fine job with the illustrations. She reads the story, gets a couple of suggestions from me, and then draws the picture. Roe has a unique gift. I am delighted that she shares it with me.

Deep gratitude is expressed to Jann Sessoms for her expertise in editing, proofing, and correcting my numerous errors. In addition, Jann provides a steady stream of emotional support for my writing. I feel greatly honored to be the recipient of her words of praise, encouragement, and affirmation.

Also, I want to express appreciation to those readers of <u>Heroes of the Heart</u> who continued to ask, "When will the second book be ready?" Indeed, you were a major influence in keeping me motivated. I thank you.

Finally, let me once again thank Martha, my wife of thirty-five years. Exercising the patience of Job, she graciously spent numerous weeknights and weekends alone while I worked on *The Book*. Martha is quite simply the easiest person to live with that I can possibly imagine. She is a great partner, companion, and friend; an awesome mother and grandmother. I'm greatly blessed in being able to share the journey with her.

Introduction

Why do people get into therapy? Why would anyone make the effort, bare their souls, and pay good money to talk to a psychiatrist, a counselor, a minister, or a psychotherapist? Because they are looking for *relief*, and they know at some level that something must change in order to get it. As Jerry Clower said in his tall tale about Marcell Ledbetter who was being attacked by a lynx, "Shoot up here amongst us, one of us has got to have some relief."

Change. Most people would say they want some changes in their lives. But the majority of the same people don't do anything to bring about those changes because they do not really believe *Change is a Choice.*

Some people spend their time cursing the darkness. Others go around turning on lights because they have come to know that change is a choice.

Some folks look at the dysfunctional pathos in their family and live in denial. Others confront it and choose to change.

Some marital partners react to their destructive marriages by playing the blame game. Others stop their cooperation with it and choose to change.

Some people look at their own lives and yearn for things to be different. They hate their jobs, want to lose weight, to be more congenial, wish they were less stressed, more patient, less depressed, less angry, more at peace. Others take charge of their lives and choose to change because change really is a choice.

Some people choose to change and are able to do it alone. Others get help, not because they're weak, but because they're strong enough to admit their weaknesses.

However, in either case, *change seldom happens until you see it as a choice and choose to make it happen.*

In some instances, change is simple and can be accomplished with very little effort. Sometimes it demands tremendous effort, requires assistance, and needs major support.

Why is that the case? Why does change come so easily for some and so hard for others?

Well, there are many reasons. Some of which include genetic wiring, the developmental process, personal life experiences, and on and on. Regardless, change comes easier when you discover *who you are, how you got that way, and learn what you can do about it when you choose to change.*

Some people seem to think change *requires a miracle.* A man said in a therapy session, "Well, I'm not saying my wife won't change, but I do know it will take a miracle. I've waited twenty years for it, and I'm not waiting any longer." But the truth is, change seldom requires a miracle or some supernatural intervention.

Some people think change automatically occurs if *enough time passes.* They often repeat: "Time heals all wounds," as if they're quoting scripture. But that well-known verse isn't in the Bible. Furthermore, it isn't true. Time alone does not heal. The passing of time may enhance burying your hurt a little deeper, and possibly you become desensitized to it. But wounds of the soul don't heal just from the passage of time.

A woman once told me, "We've got a family problem and need help. My father will not accept the man I married. He is rude and hostile toward my husband. And he won't even consider trying to work it out."

"How long have you been married?" I asked.

"Thirty years," she replied.

Well, this story is certainly not the norm, but it does illustrate my point quite favorably. The passage of time does not automatically mean change.

In addition, change *seldom happens instantly*. I know there are examples to the contrary. But those are the exceptions, not the rule. Example: You can become a Christian in an instant, but it is a lifetime project of changing in trying to become Christlike. Such radical change rarely happens instantly.

Change seldom happens as a *result of hoping it's going to get better.* I've heard countless stories of people enduring intolerable marriages, jobs, children, parents, and friends. When I ask why they have condoned something so unbearable for so long, they usually say, "I kept hoping it would get better."

Former major league baseball player and long time broadcaster, Joe Garagiola had a colorful way of calling play by play. When a pitcher was in trouble and having a hard time throwing a strike, Joe would say, "He's ready to throw his *hope* pitch. That's the one he throws and *hopes* something good will happen."

Hope pitches seldom work. In fact, baseball pitchers who throw very many *hope pitches* usually find themselves in another line of work.

My point is: *Change is a choice that requires a decision.* That does not mean change will automatically occur when you make the decision, but it is the required beginning. To put it another way, don't count on change occurring in your life until you make the decision for it. It won't happen. You can bet the family savings on it.

Throughout this volume, you will be exposed to people who have chosen to change. Some of them stopped cursing the darkness, turned on the lights, and started cleaning up the mess.

Some of the stories are about people who looked at their dysfunctional families, stopped living in denial, had appropriate confrontations, and chose to change.

Several of the pieces are about married couples. Some decided to stop cooperating with their destructive relationship by playing the blame game, and made a decision to change.

Other stories are about individuals who stopped gazing at their navels, longing for things to be different. Instead, they took charge of their lives and chose to make things change. If you want changes in your life, marriage, family, or world, I hope this book will help you stay focused on this truth: Change is a Choice.

I trust that you will choose to make it so.

Contents

Chapter 1

Ambushed on the Road Less Traveled

> "'Tis better to have loved and lost,
> than never to have loved at all."
> Tennyson

All the signs of chemotherapy were visible. Pale skin, head wrapped in a turban, walking gingerly and just a little unstable. But she had a smile that matched her clear blue eyes. From my position atop a StairMaster, I had seen her a couple of days earlier walking the exercise track at the local health club.

Each time she came around the turn with twinkling eyes, she looked over at the StairMaster machines and smiled. At first, I thought she was making eyes at me.

But observing my overweight carcass huffing and puffing and gasping for breath, I knew that couldn't be the case!

Looking to my left, I saw a dark, trim, well-conditioned man with a smile who was making eyes at her. When she came around the next time, I saw the same thing-- her eyes twinkled, and she smiled. The man next to me sent the same body language back to her.

Without thinking, I said, "How's your wife?"

"Doing pretty well, right now," he replied. "She's just finished another round of chemo."

"I know," I said.

"Do you know Penny?" he asked.

"No, but I know chemo when I see it, and I've been watching the two of you sending a lot of love energy back and forth."

He smiled and cleared his throat. "It's that obvious, huh?"

"It is to me," I said.

He began to talk.

She had been diagnosed with breast cancer and had undergone a radical mastectomy and reconstructive surgeries. Chemo had followed and things had gone well for a time. But cancer returned; more treatment followed.

When he finished his workout, she was waiting for him at the end of the track. Getting off the machine, he stuck out his hand and said, "I'm Paul. Thanks for asking and listening."

As we parted, I said, "You guys hang in there."

Over the next few weeks, that scene was repeated several times. Each time I saw Paul, I'd ask about Penny. Eagerly, he gave an update. One night, he wanted me to meet her. She was charming and delightful.

Time passed, and I was aware that I had not seen Paul in a long while. Then, one night I saw him again, and I asked how things were going.

His face strained a bit when he said, "Penny died two months ago. She'd been in the hospital for several days. She died in my arms on Thanksgiving Eve."

When he called my office a few weeks later, he said, "Got your phone number out of the yellow pages. Could I make an appointment? I'm not doing so well."

The story he told was a classic love story. It was a second marriage for both, but they were married only six years. The last three had been dominated by her illness.

Paul was ten years Penny's senior and had been divorced for twelve years before they married. He had not expected to be married again. Penny had been married to an emotionally abusive minister. She had stayed in that relationship far too long.

When Paul and Penny got together, it was magic for both. He was a *type-A*, corporate executive; hard-nosed and success-oriented. He was well-heeled and well-traveled. He knew nothing of the fine arts, spirituality, or emotional intimacy. She, on the other hand, was a classical pianist, with a soul full of spirituality, and a heart as big as Texas.

Penny had grown up in a strong and solid Tennessee family that was sensitive and supportive. They accepted Paul with open arms and he loved them dearly.

As he wined her and dined her, he delighted in fulfilling her innermost dreams. She delighted in exposing him to music, the church, and taught him how to love and be loved.

On one trip, they flew to Maui, and just as he had planned it, arrived after dark. Early the next morning, he opened the blinds in their penthouse suite and woke her to watch the sunrise over Maalaea Bay.

Penny introduced Paul to classical music and taught him about opera and the symphony. When she played piano for him, he often cried.

For their first anniversary, they went to the opera. When they returned home, Penny was shocked to find a black nine-foot Steinway standing in their living room. Resting on the top was a long-stemmed red rose.

Paul and Penny spent three years in a storybook marriage known only by a few. Then, they were *ambushed on the road less traveled.* Ambushed by cancer. That demonic intruder ransacked their lives. Predictably, what followed was: surgeries, several chemotherapy treatments, loss of hair, loss of dignity, loss of weight, excruciating pain, and all the rest.

By some measure, some would say that cancer destroyed a beautiful relationship. But not so, for Paul and Penny. Yes, they were ambushed. No, the enemy did not win the contest.

During the three years that Penny was sick, their relationship grew rather than deteriorated! The emotional intimacy they experienced went to a new depth. In spite of the grief, pain, and heartache (perhaps because of it), they grew even closer.

Telling that part of the story, Paul said, "There is no intimacy so deep as that which you experience when you openly and honestly go through dying and death together."

Paul's grief was long, hard, and difficult. Friends tried to help by suggesting that he get involved right away in another relationship. He was often offended and annoyed. He refused to use another woman to distract him from his pain. I salute him for that.

The intensity of grief is directly proportional to the measure of one's self that is invested in that which is lost.

In Paul's case, a very large part of his inner self was invested in Penny, their marriage, and their lives together. For the first time in his life, he had opened his heart completely to another. When she died, a very large part of his inner self felt mortally wounded. Thus, for Paul, the grieving process would be long and hard, and it couldn't be rushed.

During his therapy, I encouraged him to get into journaling under my direction. And he did.

My first experience with journaling (for myself) was in 1970. I've used it with clients for nearly that long. Few things can match the value of journaling to speed the healing process and spawn insights into one's life.

Using the journaling process, Paul poured out his heart on paper. He wrote without filtering or censoring. He wrote before he thought, rather than vice versa. Par for the course, he was often surprised and even shocked at what he wrote. Like other neophytes in the journaling process, he often said, "I can't believe I wrote that!"

One such surprise came the day he found himself writing that he wanted to learn to play piano. What he wrote was, "To honor the love of my life, I want to learn to play Beethoven's *Moonlight Sonata*." (She loved that piece, and he loved to hear her play it.)

When he read that part of his journal to me, he was a little embarrassed and said, "Isn't that ridiculous!? I'm forty-eight years old and never played piano in my life."

"Not ridiculous at all." I said, "When are you planning to start?"

"Today," he said.

Several months later, he played Beethoven's *Moonlight Sonata*. Not without flaw, but that wasn't the point. He played it for himself and Penny. She would have been mighty proud.

One of my assignments to him was to set aside the time to write *Penny's Story*. It took a long time for him to do that, but it was extremely therapeutic in helping him to adjust to this great loss.

It's been several years since Penny's death. During that period, in spite of his intense grief, many splendid things have occurred in Paul's life. He now owns his own business which has been enormously successful. He has been elected to a high position of service in his church. He still plays piano. He is still single. He has had some very good relationships with two or three wonderful women. However, he always backs away before things get too serious. He's afraid to open his heart so completely again. But he's still healing. Maybe someday he will. Maybe not.

Chapter 2

*Behold, A Child Shall **Disrupt** Them*

> "The best laid plans of
> mice and men..."
> Robert Burns

My sermon was entitled "Overcoming Life's Limitations." It was about coping with disappointments, hardships, and weaknesses. It was about dealing with the bumps and curves in the road that we don't choose, don't want, don't like. It was about having your train of life derailed and having to make second choices.

My Biblical reference was about the apostle Paul being shipwrecked, having to make adjustments, and the good that came out of it. I illustrated with Robert Frost.

*****

Two Roads diverged in a yellow wood.
And sorry I could not travel both.
Being one traveler, long I stood
And looked down one as far as I could,
To where it bent in the undergrowth.

Then took the other as just as fair,
And having perhaps the lesser claim,
Though really the travel there
Had worn them really about the same.

I shall be telling this with a sigh,
Somewhere ages and ages hence,
Two roads diverged in a yellow wood and I--
Took the one less traveled
And that has made all the difference.

****

During the years I was in the pastorate, on periodic occasions, I would get struck with a bad case of *dramatic fever*. This particular Sunday was one of those days.

My intention was to take my topic, "Overcoming Life's Limitations," and milk it, goad it, gouge it, knead it, apply it to every person in the house, and wring every last drop of emotion out of it. Then I would use my best illustration, work it to a fever pitch, and finish with a whispered closure.

My closing story was about the renowned violinist, Niccolo Paganini, who while playing one of his most important concerts, got to the final movement and broke a string on his violin. Yet, he finished the concert on three strings, and no one ever knew the difference.

Because he improvised, and met the challenge of his limitations, he overcame the disappointments of the occasion, and finished a beautiful concert with only three strings. **That's the way it was supposed to end.**

Now let me set the stage for this presentation. The building was *comfortably filled.* Normally, when that statement is made by a minister, it means there was enough room for everyone to lie down. But on that particular Sunday, saying the building was comfortably filled means it was a very good crowd, which pushed my adrenalin even higher.

Sitting just to my right on the front row were three ten-year-old boys who had been assigned that spot because they had been acting up in church. One of the mothers spoke to me about their misbehavior.

"Have them sit on the first row where I can keep an eye on them. That should solve the problem," I smugly surmised. But that was a bad move. A very bad move.

Actually, for a couple of weeks, it had worked out quite well. But may I remind you that on this particular Sunday my bout with dramatic fever was running high. My humdinger of a sermon was going to finish on such a high note that I expected the people to leave the building so worked up to cope with their limitations, they'd be ready to *go bear hunting with a switch.* Trust me; it was a bad move to have those boys on the front row.

You see, behavior was not the only problem with these three knuckleheads. I don't know which one of the suspects gets the credit or blame sitting there on pew #1, just off to my right. But one of them had a problem which soon became MY problem. What *was* that problem, you ask?

Well, how can I say this tactfully? I have no intention of being crude. I want to be careful not to offend anybody with this story. This is a delicate subject, but one that is long overdue and must be told.

Let's see, I could say the problem was flatulence. Or is it sensitive enough if I say the problem was gas? Maybe I'll be bold enough to call it what a dear friend called it with her first graders, "Somebody has a problem of hiney-buzzing." I'll stop there. I think you get the picture.

Well, it happened right at the most dramatic moment of my sermon, actually, right in the middle of Paganini's concert. On red oak pews, made for dignified heavenly bodies. On solid wood benches that did not have padding. Do you understand what I'm saying?!

Using a dramatic crescendo, I said, "One of the world's greatest violinists gave his most memorable concert by overcoming horrendous limitations. In the last movement of his performance, he broke his *G-string*...."

God as my witness, it didn't occur to me there would be more than one image pictured when I mentioned the broken G-string. I promise you that when I was preparing that sermon (no doubt having my head in the clouds or something worse), it did not strike me as being funny to say that Paganini broke his G-string. But it did those boys, and they snickered. One of them hiney-buzzed. It was so loud that it was picked up by the microphone on the pulpit, and recorded on tape, and is in my file to this day.

Now, I want you to know that Niccolo Paganini might have finished his concert in brilliant form on three strings, after he broke his G-string, but I was not so brilliant. I limped through the next few minutes barely audible for fear I was going to fall on the floor and break out in *holy hilarity*.

Thanks, boys, for keeping me humble. Indeed, you brought a most fitting END to my outbreak of dramatic fever.

Moral. The main reason I included that story in this volume is because... well, just because it's a great story. But more than that, it's really a metaphor for those who tend to take life (myself included) and everything in it, much too seriously.

Numerous people, with whom I work in therapy, need to keep this story and the truth it *imparts* close at hand. (Pardon the play on words, but I couldn't resist.) Few things set us up for disappointment, and hurt our feelings, more than *taking life too seriously*. Those who live life with such an attitude of intensity are *misery makers*. They make life miserable for themselves and those around them, causing everyone to miss the enjoyment of the journey.

A good case in point. A client once told me of a family vacation that occurred when he was a boy. It was a cross-country trip that included sightseeing in the mountain states. The father was an intense, uptight, totally serious individual. Due to some unexpected delays because of weather and traffic, they were running a few hours behind schedule (the travel schedule that was made out by this all-too-serious father.) So, he decided that in order to get back on the pre-planned timetable, they would just bypass the Grand Canyon!

Can you believe that? One of the world's most awesome sights was bypassed in order to stay on a stupid schedule. That, my friends, is taking life too damn seriously. That man could have benefited from having those three boys on pew #1 in the car with him!

If you're not enjoying life very much, perhaps you're taking it too seriously. Maybe you need to lean back, take a deep breath, and laugh. If you're having trouble laughing, just remember my dramatic sermon that was disrupted by the hiney-buzzing. Maybe it will help you as much as it did me.

Chapter 3

Never Try To Teach A Pig To Dance

> "Vulnerability is the window through which blows the warm breeze of pleasure and the cold wind of pain."   Author

"What's the most common cause of marital conflict?" That question has been posed to me many times. My standard response is-- **Excessive Expectations.**

Unconsciously, many people expect their partners to fix their childhood wounds. That's one of the things that draws people to marriage. It's also what draws them to the one they choose. The problem is two-fold:

First, **you can never make up for what you missed**

in childhood through adult relationships. Nor can you off-set childhood damage through adult relationships. Until we learn that, we continue with our excessive expectations.

Second, **you can never get enough of what you don't need.** If the child within you has an unhealed wound, your mate cannot fix it. But if you are unconsciously expecting that to happen, criticism of the mate usually follows.

"You don't kiss me enough."

"You don't love me enough."

In addition to criticism, trying to control the mate joins the scenario.

"I don't want you to work."

" I want you to be home when I get home."

After exercising *criticism* and *control*, a vigorous attempt to *change* the mate can't be far away.

"I want you to be more outgoing, more involved in civic affairs, wear better clothes."

Trying to change a mate into something he/she is not, makes about as much sense as *trying to teach a pig to dance.* You can count on it-- *it will frustrate the pig and make you very angry!* Invariably, it leads to resentment, depression, withdrawal, accusations, or all of the above:

"You're not meeting my needs."

"You don't really love me."

"You don't love me as much as I love you."

"You never..."

"You always..."

"Maybe this marriage isn't going to work."

"Maybe I picked the wrong person."

"Leave me alone."
"Nothing I do pleases you."
"What do you want me to do?"
"What do you want me to say?"

The cycle is vicious. Such was the case of Marie, and her scenario of love. Said she, "When I fall in love with a man, I'm just sure he's my *one and only*. Then, it gets more intense, and I love everything about him. I think about him all the time, and want to spend every minute with him. I love making love to him. Next, I start wanting more than he's giving of his time, attention, and sex. I begin to resent him, just a little. Then, a lot. Then, I become hostile. I pick fights because he's not giving enough. Finally, I split with him and end up hating him."

Sound familiar? Marie had repeated this cycle numerous times. She clearly proved the maxim: *You can never get enough of what you don't need.*

Does that mean it's hopeless? Yes, it probably is hopeless, *until you get past the place of blaming the partner for your feelings.* Unless you focus on the relationship (rather than the mate) and get honest about what has made it what it is, there's not much hope.

Marriage is one of life's greatest paradoxes-- *it's the source of life's greatest pleasure and the source of life's greatest pain.* Frequently, the same relationship is the source of both experiences. Doesn't make sense, does it? Maybe it does.

A great relationship that produces intense pleasure is the byproduct of emotional intimacy. It comes through being open, honest, and vulnerable (which is perhaps the most important of all.) Vulnerability is the window through which blows the warm breeze of pleasure and the cold wind of pain.

In fact, you can't have it both ways-- open to the pleasure and protected from the pain. Intimacy is not a semi-permeable membrane that lets the pleasure through and filters out the pain.

When you have accepted in your head and heart that intimacy involves pleasure and pain, you've taken a giant step. At that point, you're probably ready to deal with relational enemy #1-- excessive expectations.

There's a lot to be learned from that old redneck aphorism: "Never try to teach a pig to dance. It'll frustrate the pig and make you very angry!"

In relational therapy, I see a lot of frustration and anger resulting when one or both is trying to make the other into a dancing pig.

An abundance of peace will emerge in almost any relationship when you learn to accept each other and enjoy each other's strengths, and stop the insanity of trying to make the other into something they're not.

Never try to teach a pig to dance is the country version of Niebuhr's classic prayer:

> God grant me the serenity,
> To accept the things I cannot change,
> The courage to change the things I can,
> And the wisdom to know the difference.

Chapter 4

Looking For a Home

"So it's home again, and home again
.... for me. My heart is turning home
again, and there I long to be."
Henry Van Dyke

For eight full years, we lived in beautiful Northern California, fifteen miles from San Francisco on the mid-peninsula. The wonderful community known as Burlingame was where we made our home.

When we moved there, all three of our kids were school age. Matt was beginning tenth grade; Leanne sixth grade; and Chad second grade. By the time we left, Matt was an upper classman at the University of

Tennessee, Knoxville.   Leanne was finishing her freshman year at Cal State Fresno, and Chad had completed his first year at Burlingame High School.

Moving is seldom easy for anyone; certainly not for children. But moving when you're starting tenth grade may be the worst of all. Such was the case for Chad.

For the rest of us, living in California had been *a part of our lives*.   For Chad it had been *his life*. From second grade to tenth grade, he had been a California kid, and he loved it.

The day I told him we were moving is not one of the cherished memories of his childhood-- for him or me. To break the news, I chose to take him on a walk.

"Chad," I began, "what's the worst thing that could happen to a fifteen-year-old boy?"

"Parents get a divorce," he responded instantly.

"What's the second worst?"

"Moving."

"Chad, your mother and I are not getting a divorce." With fear in his voice, he asked, "Are we moving?"

"Yes we are."

"Shoot," he said. "Shoot. Shoot. Shoot." He kicked the ground and started to cry. "SHOOT, SHOOT, SHOOT," he said, louder and louder. (That's not exactly what he said, but it's pretty close.) We kept walking.

Finally, he said, "Where are we moving?"

As I held him and we both cried, I told him where we were moving and why.

Four months later, we watched the North American moving van pull away from our English Tudor home in Burlingame, California. Within a couple of hours, we locked the door at 1109 Cabrillo, pointed our three vehicles South on Highway 101, and began the 2500 mile trip to Memphis, Tennessee.

Arriving five days later at the attorney's office, we signed the papers and closed the deal on our new house in Germantown, Tennessee.

As the final checks were exchanged and the papers signed, I said to the closing attorney, "How long have you been doing this?"

"Twenty-two years," he beamed.

"During that period, how many times have you closed a house deal for a married couple when the husband had not seen the house?"

"To my knowledge, never."

"Then make note that this is your first one," I said. "Martha came back about a month ago and found the house and made the deal on it. I still haven't seen it."

He shook his head in surprise.

"Well," I said, "You've probably got another first coming. Can someone from your office escort us to the house? She can't remember how to get there!"

After the laughter subsided, he acknowledged that, too, was a first.

It was August 1, 1987. We had three weeks before school began to get Chad ready for tenth grade.

Germantown High School was and is one of the finest high schools in the country. And, it was big! With over 3300 students, it was almost three times the size of Burlingame High School where Chad had gone his freshman year.

On the first day of classes, as I dropped Chad off in

front of the building, I gave him a hug and a high-five. With dental braces carefully concealed, he forced a slight smile. He closed the car door, and with sack-lunch in hand, began the long walk into GHS where he did not know a single solitary soul.

When I picked him up that afternoon, the first thing he did was open the sack-lunch.

Afraid to hear the answer, I asked, "Son, why didn't you eat your lunch?"

"I didn't see anyone I wanted to sit with, and I was embarrassed to sit by myself."

"So, what did you do during the lunch period?"

"Just walked around, till it was over," he said, forcing back the tears.

"Tomorrow will be better," I prophesied. But I wasn't convincing, nor convinced. Neither was he.

Picking him up the second day, I immediately noticed the sack-lunch was gone. He had thrown it in the trash and continued to walk around during lunch. The third and fourth days were the same. On the fifth day, he sat by himself. But this was Friday; time for football. Things were bound to get better.

Martha and I took him to the game, but he spent the whole game sitting with us. This was more than we could take. Our kid was not connecting with anybody at this new school. He was grieving and depressed. Something had to be done.

Martha called the school. With a lot of charm and bull-headed tenacity (both of which she possesses in abundance), she persuaded the assistant principal to provide her with the names and phone numbers of all new transfer students in the tenth grade. There were more than one hundred. By choosing only those who had transferred from outside the Memphis area, we narrowed the list down to seventy. We split the list and began making calls.

Talking to parents and students, we invited these displaced kids to our home for a pizza party on Friday night before the next football game. At game time, they would be transported together to the stadium. Enthusiasm from the parents was high. We weren't so sure about the kids.

To our utter surprise, thirty-one showed up. What a testimony to the loneliness they were feeling! Nearly half of those we called came to a party given by someone they didn't know because they were so needy of having some peer contact.

Fifteen is an awkward age that is filled with growing pains. Too young to drive; too old to be driven. Too young to date; too old not to. Too young to make your own decisions; too old not to. Too young to have good social skills; too old not to.

So, thirty-one all-of-the-above-fifteen-year-olds came to our party and *stood around looking at each other*. The music was playing; nobody danced. The pizza was on the tables; little was being eaten. The kids were there; nothing was happening. What **was** happening in abundance was tension, awkwardness, and uneasiness. I decided to do something even if it was wrong.

Walking out on the patio and turning off the music, I said, "We really appreciate all of you coming. We're glad you're here. I have a couple of questions I'd like to ask.

So, would you get in a circle and find a place to sit?"

"How many of you hate Germantown High School?" All hands went up.

"How many of you think they're unfriendly, rude, and a bunch of snobs?" Again all hands went up. (I knew the GHS kids were not rude, unfriendly, or snobs. But, I also knew when you're fifteen, and grieving over moving, and feeling like an outsider, that's the way you perceive those around you.)

"How many of you didn't want to leave your old high school?" I was still batting a thousand.

"How many have thought (at least a little) about running away?" Several hands went up. Not all.

"One last question. How many have skipped lunch at least once because you didn't have anyone to sit with?" About two-thirds raised their hands.

"Okay, I want everybody who has the first lunch period to walk over by the ping pong table. Second lunch period by the swing set. Third lunch period by the back door. Fourth lunch period under the oak tree. Tell each other who you are, where you came here from, and make arrangements for where you're going to meet Monday for lunch."

After a few minutes, I asked them to rearrange themselves in the circle, and we continued the group exercise.

I said, "Tell us your name, where you lived before moving to Germantown, and what your old high school was like. Then, I want you to tell something about the day you moved, or something about the moving trip. It can be sad or glad, serious or funny, and everyone has to talk for at least two minutes. Well, you don't have to, but we'd like it if you would." And they did.

They told their stories. They laughed nervously. They wept silently. Some held back tears, others didn't. They interacted beautifully.

By the time we finished, they were talking freely, and obviously more relaxed. There was even some laughter that wasn't totally forced. Actually, the guys were chuckling and the girls were giggling, which I thought was a good sign.

When the time was right, they piled in the cars, driven by adult volunteers, and went to the football game-- with somebody to sit with other than parents!

For several weeks, it was common for Martha and me to have someone approach us and say, "Isn't Chad Doyle your son?" Then, they would thank us for the party.

Even though it was more than ten years ago, to this day, periodically, someone will mention that experience to us.

What happened to Chad? He worked through his grief and grew to love Germantown High School. We were greatly relieved. Several of those he met that Friday evening have remained friends to this day.

From my observations, in grief related situations, young children and teenagers are often neglected. Whether the loss involves death, divorce, or relocation, it is all too easy to let grieving children slip through the cracks.

Over the years, I've heard middle-aged adults tell heart rending stories about childhood losses that had never healed. Mainly because they were ignored or discounted, those wounds had never mended and in shocking ways had affected their lives forever.

*****

Since that experience with Chad in 1987, at the beginning of every new school year, for at least a fleeting moment, I find myself wondering how many displaced tenth graders are walking around during lunch because they have no one to sit with.

Chapter 5

Which Child Do You Love Best?

> "No two people grow up in
> the same family." Author

Quite simply, Billy Chan was one of the most unusual people I've ever met. He had a brilliant brain, a winsome personality, an eagerness to learn, and a willingness to change. He was also bipolar which is commonly known as manic-depressive.

In his manic stage he was outgoing, jolly, laughed a lot, and was very creative. Sometimes when he was manic, he got out of control and would get much too high. In that stage, Billy would act like someone using *speed or crank.* As someone put it, "He was so high he could go duck hunting with a rake." That's when he would lose perspective and get into trouble. When he was depressed, he was nearly non-functional. But, when we could keep the edge off of the highs and lows, he was a rare individual with enormous potential.

Let me get historical about Billy Chan. He was Chinese, born and raised in Taiwan. He came to the states to study physics at a great American university. Although he could hardly speak English, he earned a PhD in the minimum time allotted. After finishing his program, he went back to Taiwan to work in his father's highly successful industrial plant.

After returning home, his manic-depressive condition worsened. That's when he came for intensive therapy, having been referred by someone who knew of our program. He was a delight to work with, and the stories I could tell about this man are numerous. I will confine myself to a few.

During one session, I asked Billy about his family business. He said, "Don, in Taiwan, only find two classes of people-- vedy rich and vedy poor. My fadder, vedy rich man. You know rich, Don?"

"Yes, Billy, I understand rich."

"In Taiwan, many rich people drive Loys Loyce, and Benz. You know Loys and Benz, Don?"

"Yes, Billy, I know Rolls Royce and Mercedes Benz. I don't drive either one, but I know them."

"Don, my fadder drive new Loys. Every year, new Loys. My fadder, vedy rich man."

"Billy, how did he gain his wealth?" I asked.

"My fadder manufacture insulation padding for ski clothing. You know insulation, Don?"

"Yes, I know insulation."

"For many years, my fadder make one square yard of insulation and sell for three dollars to use in ski clothing. Then, my fadder not doing so well. One day my fadder have good idea. His insulation can be used for brassiere padding. You know brassiere padding, Don?"

"Yes, Billy, I know brassiere padding."

"Well, my fadder make one square yard of insulation to make brassiere padding for twenty five brassieres and sell for twenty five dollars. Now, my fadder very rich man."

"Oh, I see," I said. "Indeed, I understand why your father definitely is vedy rich man."

Billy worked with his father in manufacturing brassiere padding. He made a lot of money. But, he was not a happy man. His manic-depression plagued him. His highs were very high, and his lows were very low.

Current evidence strongly supports that bi-polar disorder is caused by a chemical imbalance and can be treated with proper medication. I do not question this conclusion and frequently refer clients with this condition for psychiatric evaluation. I also support the usage of medication for treatment. However, having worked with many people who have been diagnosed as manic-depressives, I have noted something quite interesting. All seem to have at least one thing in common. During childhood, the messages they received were extreme contrasts. Such as:

"You're wonderful." (or) "You're awful."

"You're a genius." (or) "You're stupid."
"I'm lucky to have you."(or) "You're a burden."
"You're good." (or) "You're bad."
"I love you." (or) "I hate you."

No grey. No middle ground. One extreme or the other. Sometimes these messages have come from the same parent. Sometimes one type came from one parent, and the other type from the other parent. But, in all cases of high/low personalities (with manic-depressive being the worst form), they seem to have experienced the same sharp contrasts in parental messages.

Let me point out that such damage is not restricted to parents. Of course, we know teachers, coaches, siblings, and extended family members can also be sources of major self-image damage. But I'm referring to the sharp contrasting messages that can come from these sources.

A child whose teacher, coach, sibling, grandparent, or authority figure changes in an instant from profuse praise to callous criticism may experience severe self-image damage. This may produce an adult with a high/low personality, possibly even manic-depressive.

Billy Chan was no exception. In fact, his story was the most bizarre contrast of extremes I've ever heard.

Billy was unusually smart. He was perhaps nearly a genius. He constantly heard messages that verified it. But a family tragedy that occurred when Billy was four brought the negative messages in spades.

Billy's brother, who was three years older, died of some unidentified disease. His mother's religious beliefs were mostly superstitious witchcraft and fallacious black magic. She concluded her first-born son's death was caused by the "evil spirit" of her second son, Billy. She blamed Billy for his brother's death, and repeatedly told him so. To make sure he never forgot it, twice a year (on the birth date and death date) she took him to the grave of his brother to confess his sin!

So, Billy Chan spent his childhood repeatedly hearing these two sharply contrasting messages: "You're a genius," (therefore wonderful.) "You're an evil spirited murderer," (therefore despicable.) If that won't make a manic-depressive out of you, I don't know what will!

One day Billy said to my wife, who worked in our office, "Martha, which one of your children do you love best?"

In predictable fashion, she responded, "Billy, I don't love any one of them *best*. I love them each the same."

With a big laugh, Billy responded, "You lie. You Americans are all alike. You say you love your children the same. But you love one best. Which one?"

Martha maintained her neutral position. So, Billy told her his story. After hearing his awful experience, she understood why he was so adamant in believing that parents love one child best.

Billy Chan had spent his entire life living in torment believing: (1)that his parents loved his dead brother much more than they loved him; (2)that the "wrong child died"; (3) worst of all, they had blamed him for the death.

Billy worked hard in therapy. Ever so slowly but surely, he began a new journey with the edge taken off his highs and lows. He learned some management techniques, and some solid healthy self-talk. He is much more whole and a lot more balanced.

He is vedy rich man.

Chapter 6

"I Shave My Legs For This?!"

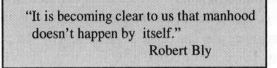

> "It is becoming clear to us that manhood
> doesn't happen by itself."
> Robert Bly

That's what she said. And you can trust me; it was an exclamation, not a question. JoAnn delivered her zinger as the capstone of a thirty-minute rebuttal. Her opening remarks had been basically free of emotion as she stated her case. She had volunteered to speak first in the session, their first ever in marital therapy.

As she put it, "It seems only fair for me to go first since this is really my idea. Roger came only because I begged him."

In a matter-of-fact manner, JoAnn served up a half-dozen morsels that troubled her about their ten-year relationship. She was clear, concise, and noticeably free of emotion. When she finished, she smiled, and with her hand gestured to Roger. It was his turn.

Roger began his defense. JoAnn listened patiently as he explained having five jobs in ten years, with the past year being unemployed. Roger concluded: "You've got a good job; so what's the big deal?"

JoAnn didn't interrupt as he countered her charges that he had a drinking problem. Yes, he drank every night and sometimes got belligerent. But it was his way of relaxing. Besides, "What's the big deal about a man taking a DRANK, now and then?"

She squirmed a bit when he answered her charges that he had neglected their three children, and left all the parenting to her. He explained that parenting was a woman's job. Besides, "You're the one that wanted kids; so what's the big deal?"

JoAnn's countenance and posture began to change when Roger moved into his **A** material. Her face flushed and her lips pursed when Roger began to talk about their sexual problems.

"Doc, she didn't bring it up, but I know she's going to. So, I just want to get this out and done with. Two or three times, when I had a little too much to drink, and she resisted me sexually, I popped her. Not hard and never with a closed fist. Just two or three times over a ten-year period, I slapped her. But I never really hurt her; so what's the big deal?"

"And I know she's gonna bring this up, too, so I just

as well to get this out in the open. Yes, to try to help her get over her prudishness, I have insisted that she watch porno movies with me. Don't seem like a big deal to me! And twice, maybe three times, when I was drunk, and she made me mad, I guess you could say I tried to force her to have sex. Never successfully, I might add; so, what's the big deal?"

Without taking a breath, he gave his defense for her charges of infidelity. Yes, he had been involved with a few women over the years. But no more than his buddies. It was "just a thing guys do." He wanted to be accepted for "who he was." Those other women had done that for him. The women meant nothing to him. Roger finished his litany with gusto, "Besides, if you weren't so rigid, frigid, and prudish, I wouldn't fool around; so what's the big deal?"

When he finished his defense, Roger folded his arms, and sat back in the leather chair. Smugly, he looked at me as if I were a domestic judge who was prepared to say, "Not Guilty."

My guess was he thought that I, as another man, would surely be on his side and come to his defense. Little did he know that I not only grew up around that kind of male trash, but I had also spent a career challenging such stupidity.

During Roger's exhortation, it had been quite obvious that JoAnn had done okay listening to him counter all her concerns about everything except the sexual issue. That's when he crossed the line. Observing her body language, I thought to myself, "When she came in here, she only had one nerve left. And he just got on it!"

No doubt about it, Roger was shocked when I turned to JoAnn and said, "Would you like to respond to this chauvinistic, sexist, testosterone-laden b.s.? Do you want to tell your husband what the big deal is?" And she did.

She was hot. Her eyes danced and arms waved as she unloaded her dirty laundry list of disappointments, resentments, and unhappiness.

"Roger?" she asked. "Do you want to know what the big _____deal is? Well, I'm gonna tell you what the big _____ deal is!"

For the next several minutes, she spoke rapidly and emotionally. Listening to her, I was reminded that the Brazilians explain suppression of feelings by saying, "Put a rock on it." It was clear, the rock had just been lifted from JoAnn's quarry.

She said, "Roger, you're about as romantic as an empty glass of buttermilk." Then she said his lovemaking skills were no better than the redneck whose idea of foreplay was to say, "Brace yourself, Betty Lou." She continued by saying, "Your drunken sloppy kisses are like kissing a plate of spaghetti." Then she added, "Sex with you is like singing a song in four-part harmony-- get it up, get it in, get it off, get it out." She finished her diatribe by saying, "You're not a man; you're a mouse. And you've made a mouse out of me. But I'm getting out of the trap, and you can keep the cheese."

After a moment of silence, she looked at me, gestured to the side with both hands, and in exasperation and disgust, made a statement I had never heard before. "I shave my legs for this?!"

Biting my lip to keep from laughing, I said, "Perhaps,

you'd like to elaborate?"

She said, "Can you imagine wanting to **be** a woman, **look** like a woman, **act** like a woman for a piece of work like that? I can't believe I've tolerated this crap for ten years. Well, not anymore, honey. Not anymore. I'm not shaving my legs for that abuse anymore!"

Looking at Roger, I could see he was still alive. His face was a little pale, but I could tell he was breathing. So, I proceeded.

Actually, at this point, I had just seen the second sign of optimism. At least one of the two was ready to be honest and open about feelings! The first sign had come during the opening moments of the session when I had asked, "Is divorce an option?" Both had answered in the affirmative-- divorce was an option. Strange as it may seem, coming from a (Christian) marital therapist, that is a positive sign. Let me explain.

When a couple insists that divorce is not an option, more often than not, the therapy will do little more than place a Band-Aid on a gaping wound. They will deal only with the SYMPTOM and not the CAUSE. And they will go off to do a little better for a little while. But the real problem will return, and so will the marital discord.

When I ask if divorce is an option and both answer, "No," I will often say, "Then I suggest you not waste your money and my time."

So, when one or both say that divorce is an option, I see that as an optimistic sign that maybe, just maybe, they will invest the time, energy, and money to make some major changes which can produce unusually good results.

Let me elaborate on this issue. The high rate of

divorce in our culture is generally looked on as extremely negative, and a sign of everything that is wrong with our society. However, I find it disturbing to unequivocally label divorce with such negativity.

In my opinion, in numerous instances, divorce is a very positive sign of the times. In many cases, it means that married people (particularly women) will not take the torment anymore. They will not continue living with abuse and call it "the way men are." They will not take a grossly distorted Biblical teaching (regarding marriage) and thereby tolerate an otherwise intolerable situation.

The same sort of irrational thinking is used to promote *the man is the head of the house issue*. It is very interesting to me to observe that many Christian women, who teach and preach that the man should be the head of the house, are in fact living in a relationship where it is obvious they (the wives) are the dominant partner. Professionally, or personally, I find absolutely nothing wrong with the wife being the dominant partner, except for the obvious hypocrisy and blatant denial.

QUESTION. Who should be the HEAD of the house?

ANSWER. The one with the best leadership qualities and skills. In most cases, in its healthiest form, the leader changes constantly depending on who is the best at what.

The idea that the husband (because he has the X and Y chromosome) should always have the final word is irrational indoctrination at best. At worst, it's just plain stupid. It's a teaching that is based on myth and comes from grossly insecure men who quite often have *female trouble*-- their own mothers!

In the name of God, when will we stop using the Holy

Scriptures to trap people in relationships that are unreasonable and demonic? In the name of God, when will we stop?!

If you interpret this to mean that I am a promoter of divorce, you have missed my point entirely. My clients will attest to the fact that I almost never give up on a marital relationship. In fact, there are times when I have erred in not giving more support, and perhaps some would say, *permission* to terminate. No, my point is not to *promote* divorce. But I do believe divorce is sometimes, dare I say, many times, the loving, Christian, thing to do.

The high divorce rate in today's society is very complex, and has many components. Without question, the massive breakup of families is extremely damaging to modern culture. However, in my opinion, it is grossly unfair to lump all divorce together as ultimately wrong. Sometimes, it is the lesser of two evils.

Frequently, modern divorce reflects that women are no longer willing to live their lives through a patriarchal model. They are not willing to be dominated, denigrated, and dehumanized by abusive, insensitive, insecure little boys who are posing as men. From my perspective, divorce in that setting is the lesser of the two evils, and should be supported rather than opposed.

Meanwhile, back to JoAnn and Roger. Since both had said divorce *was* an option, I registered that as a sign of optimism. Now, in addition, at least one had opened up with honesty and emotion, which was optimism sign number two. I was encouraged and pressed on.

(To be continued in following chapter)

Chapter 7

"I Shave My Legs For This?!" Part II

> "Sex is paradoxical. It's the source
> of some of life's greatest pleasure
> and its greatest pain."   Author

Using JoAnn and Roger from the previous chapter as our backdrop, let's talk about sex.

Sexuality is one of the most complex aspects of the psycho/socio/spiritual developmental processes. With as much exposure as we have to sex through every avenue of media, it is amazing how much ignorance and bad information is still prevalent. Sexual therapy invariably includes a great deal of *unlearning*.

In a therapy session several years ago, a woman was complaining to her husband about their sex life. She said he was a poor performer and didn't take her sexual needs seriously. She topped it off by turning to me and saying, "It's so bad, I haven't had an *organism* in years!"

Well, quite honestly I didn't know whether to sympathize with her or congratulate her. I do know she could have used a little sexual unlearning.

She was not unlike the man who needed some extensive *unlearning* who applied for a job with my brother Chris. Filling out the application, he did fine with the first three questions. As you will see, the next two were quite different:

(1) Name?	Billy Jack Doe
(2) Address?	1111 Acorn, Jackson, TN
(3) Birthday?	10/20/61
(4) Nearest relative?	About two miles.
(5) Sex?	About twice a month.

The two people in our story were not quite that bad, but they didn't miss it by much. Fortunately, they were quick studies and eager to make progress. And they did.

Over a period of time, JoAnn and Roger disclosed who they were, and how they got that way. They responded well when I offered some guidelines on how to change if they chose to. I'd like to share their stories with you.

As you read these narratives, keep this in mind: *Children have their **gender** validated by the opposite gender parent, and their **sexuality** modeled by the parent of the same gender.*

Example. A little girl learns from her father that he is

glad that she is a female child; she learns from her mother how to be a woman. Conversely, a mother conveys to her son that she's glad he is a boy child; he learns from his father how to be a man.

With this in mind, let me introduce this couple.

First, let's get to know Roger. He wasn't a bad guy, just confused and insecure. His dad was critical and harsh, especially with Roger. Dad had never met a woman he didn't DISLIKE, and said so with regularity. Something was wrong with every woman who crossed his path, especially his wife, Roger's mother.

Through example, Dad had taught that women were to be used, and if necessary, abused. "Sometimes," he was fond of saying, "A woman has to be put in her place with a backhand across the chops!" Afterward, he'd usually laugh, clear his throat, and grin smugly.

Everyone in the family knew Dad had affairs with other women. In fact, when Roger was young, Dad often took him along as a cover for his liaisons. He threatened Roger not to tell, which Roger remembered all too well.

To offset Dad's harsh and critical behavior, Roger's mom succumbed to the temptation of numerous mothers. She over-compensated. She spoiled him is what she did. She gave him everything he wanted, and she never said "no" to anything.

Frequently, she told him, "You will always be Mama's little prince."

As Roger remembered these details, he always got emotional and often started coughing. I figured it was psychosomatic, as mother equaled *smother*.

So here's the deal with Roger. His mother certainly

validated his gender. She loved that he was a boy child, but she overdid it, which produced very unhealthy results. Dad had taught him how to be a man by being insensitive to women, and using them for sex, which never gave him a clue about emotional intimacy.

All of this produced a man who viewed sex as a hormonal function, viewed a wife primarily as a mother, and viewed himself as deserving whatever he wanted, whenever he wanted, with whomever he wanted. Is that a good prospect for a healthy marriage partner? Any woman that signs on for that is going to have a full plate!

Now let's get to know likeable, lovable JoAnn. She was clean as a hound's tooth, right? Hardly. JoAnn was a charmer, for sure. She was well-mannered, energetic, classy, and just flirtatious enough to be subtly seductive. Her pithy statements and cliches added to her charisma. All of this neatly covered the glitches in her armor. Her story?

JoAnn's father had never validated her gender. He was fond of saying, "Both my boys are girls." Then he would laugh. And others would laugh. JoAnn didn't laugh. Although she never really identified it as rejection, she always knew her father had really wanted a boy. As the last child, she had been the final disappointment.

Looking to her mother for clues on being a woman, JoAnn got a very clear message. Men will always pester you about sex. You should never show you are interested or enjoy it. Look sensuous, but not too sexy, and men will always follow you around and drool. That's the way men are. Flirt with them, but keep them at arm's length, and you can stay in control. So, what do you get with a package like that? You get a woman who needed affection and gender validation, but one who is very inhibited and uncomfortable with being a sexual woman.

What JoAnn needed from a man was a *father* who would hold her, nurture her, cuddle, and coddle her. This prompted her to view sex as the price a woman pays for being held. She reminded me of a very promiscuous woman who said in a group therapy session, "I've traded a lot of sex for a few measly hugs."

So, JoAnn and Roger were trying to have a sexually fulfilling marriage with six people in the bed-- the two of them and both sets of parents. That's a tough assignment! A tough assignment, indeed. That's like trying to make love with a mattress between you. Probably . . . *ain't gonna work.*

Well, you'll be pleased to know that JoAnn and Roger were quick studies. After discovering the truth, they were eager to work on it. They made great progress. They took seriously my assurance: *The Truth Will Set You Free, But First It Will Make You Miserable.* Their lives are better, and their marriage has remarkably improved.

To achieve this much-improved relationship, both JoAnn and Roger spent some time in Purgatory Corner. (At DFCC, that's the place where purging, cleansing, and healing take place.) As a result, each came to accept, understand, and apply to their relationship several things about sex. These included:

(1) Sexuality is one of life's greatest paradoxes. It is simple, yet complex.

(2) Sex is the source of some of life's greatest pleasure, **and** some of life's greatest pain.

(3) Our society is inundated with sexual stuff from every direction. Yet, for most couples, it is still very difficult to openly and honestly talk about it.

(4) Copulating is natural. Making love has to be learned. For most couples, the learning curve effectively starts after **unlearning** a great deal.

(5) Sex is a paradox. It's an experience that should be reserved for adulthood, yet everything about our sexual self-image was learned in childhood.

(6) *Feminine sex* needs a reason to have sex. *Masculine sex* just needs a place. Yet, both men and women have masculine and feminine sides, and both need to express and experience each form of sexuality.

(7) *Recreational* sex is hormonal. *Relational* sex is emotional. Men and women have a need for both.

(8) There are several legitimate reasons to engage in sex, making love is one of them.

(9) After getting some sexual healing, by dealing with childhood sexual baggage, couples can learn to apply these truths to their relationship.

(10) Dealing with the REAL problem of sexual discord, and not just the symptoms, takes a lot of effort, energy, and determination.

To embark on such a journey can produce results that are well worth the investment. Ask Roger. He's never felt so loved, nor acted so loving. Ask JoAnn. She'll gladly shave her legs for that.

Chapter 8

"Is There a Doctor in the House?"

> "Older men declare war. But it is youth that must fight and die....and inherit the tribulation, the sorrow, and the aftermath of war."   Herbert Hoover

The morning worship service was well underway. Hymns had been sung, prayers said, and the organist and choir had stirred our souls. At about 11:20, our souls moved from stirred to shocked. Just as one of the ministers was beginning the announcements, a man on the front row let out a scream that startled us all. (I had always suspected that many parishioners had wanted to scream during the announcements. However, this was a little more than I had envisioned.) When he let out a second and third agonizing cry, we knew he was serious!

Stumbling toward the chancel, he fell flat on the floor. One might have thought he was taking literally a line from the old hymn, "...let angels prostrate fall..."

However, the possibility of angelic presence was completely dismissed as his blood-curdling scream continued. At the top of his lungs, he yelled, "Medic! MEDIC! **MEDIC**!"

The congregation went totally silent. So did the elders, ushers, and clergy. For a few moments, everyone in the building seemed paralyzed. We watched as a wild man screamed out his pain.

The ministers looked toward me with pleading eyes. I whispered, "I'm your guest. I wouldn't want to intrude on your pastoral duties!" They were not amused.

When the senior minister finally moved toward the tormented man, others followed. At first he yelled louder and swung his fists in protest. The minister persisted in his attempt to communicate. The organist began to play and the congregation sang-- without enthusiasm.

He was still face-down on the marble floor and sobbing uncontrollably. The minister whispered something to an usher. In a rush, he went down the aisle, and motioned to a man in the pews. The worshiper responded; going directly to the screaming man's side.

Miraculously, in just a few moments, this hysterical human being was leaving the building with his arm around the one who was summoned for assistance.

Watching this happen, I was thinking: "Lucky there was a doctor in the house. Must have given him an injection of a powerful tranquilizer. That guy must have been a doper on a bad trip. After all, this is downtown

Los Angeles. Crazy people walk the streets. Some walk into churches. Lucky for us, and this vagabond, there was a doctor in the house."

Well, it's time to fess up. I was wrong. My thoughts and feelings were insensitive and stereotypical. I was dead wrong. And I was ashamed.

The man on the floor was a Vietnam veteran who was having a flashback. Something in one of the hymns had triggered an awful memory of death and dying.

Vietnam. That dreadful scar on American history where more than 56,000 Americans died. But the end of the war didn't end the tragedy. More than 100,000 have committed suicide since they came home. Who could guess how many more self-inflicted deaths were not identified as such?

No, this hysterical young man wasn't wild or crazy at all. He was just screaming out his torment on the marble floor in God's house. Nor was it a doctor who came to his aid. He was a fellow Vietnam veteran who had dealt with his own pain, and was now trained to help others deal with theirs. He gave no injection or tranquilizer. He had learned how to use his *gift of experience* to help others.

What he did was really quite simple. Touching him gently on the shoulder, all he said was, "I know, my friend. I was there, too. I know. I care. Let's go talk about it."

Wow!

******

In my experience, peer counseling is one of the most effective avenues of healing. There's something powerful about working through your own issues, and then developing the skills to help others deal with theirs. Self-help groups such as Alcoholic Anonymous and other Twelve Step programs are good examples of the effectiveness of peer counseling.

Unfortunately, just having been through a certain experience or tragedy doesn't automatically give one the tools to become an effective peer counselor. Prime example. Some women who had a bad experience in giving birth, will often scare the Bejesus out of other first-time pregnant women. That's not a sexist statement, it's just a reality. Men are equally capable of doing the same type thing.

So, having had a certain experience, trauma, or tragedy does not automatically make one a good peer counselor. However, taking the time and making the effort to learn how to use your *gift of experience* to pave the way for helping others can be extremely valuable.

Over the years, I've led many weekend seminars on the topic of "Peer Counselor Training." Sometimes we've called it, "Help Yourself by Helping Others." On some occasions, it's been known as "Common Cup Crisis Intervention."

In the ten hours of training, we listen, learn, and practice. We learn how to be an empathic listener, and how to respond to unanswerable questions. We learn what to ask, what not to ask, what to say, and what not to say. And we practice. And we practice. The experience is always exhilarating to me.

One of my major mentors in the area of peer counseling was a man I knew only from a distance. Carlyle Marney wrote a book entitled, <u>Priests to Each Other</u>. I read it in 1972. It changed my life.

Marney's premise was that the followers of Christ were *called* to be helpers and counselors to each other, thus priests. In every church service, he said, there should be "a priest at every elbow."

In 1974, I met the man himself. I was attending a conference in a large hotel where Dr. Marney was a guest speaker. As I stepped into an elevator, he was already on board. Spontaneously, I stuck out my hand, gave my name, and said, "Dr. Marney, you've been my long time hero. I really appreciate all your writings, and I want you to know <u>Priests to Each Other</u> changed my life."

Shaking my hand, he asked, "Don, what do you do?"

"I'm a pastor down in South Georgia."

"South Georgia. That's God's country. Reminds me of Sidney Lanier and <u>The Marshes of Glynn</u>. Don Doyle, what's *pressing you* down in God's country in South

Georgia?" he asked. His deep voice resonated genuine concern.

"Oh, just the usual I guess," I said, dancing a little side step. "Probably not any different than other pastors."

"I'll bet it gets very lonely down there at times, doing the work of a pastor and all?" he said. His words and tone conveyed more of a question than a statement.

"Well, yes, as a matter of fact, it is kinda lonely at times," I said, being more honest with an answer.

"Well, Don Doyle, I bet you're doing a good job of being a pastor in South Georgia," he said as he put his arm around me, and gave me a shoulder squeeze.

The elevator had now stopped on the ground floor, and we were moving toward the lobby.

"Thanks again, Dr. Marney," I said, moving away.

"Don Doyle," he said, "are you in a hurry? I'd like you to meet my wife. She's in the gift shop."

"No hurry at all," I said, hardly able to believe what I was hearing.

"Do you have dinner plans?" he asked. "We'd like you to join us."

Dinner plans, I thought?! Are you kidding me? This man, who has been my hero from a distance, whom I've just met on an elevator, has just invited me to dinner?! I didn't have any plans, but believe me, even if I had, they would have been instantly changed.

The man's message and his actions were congruent. The added bonus-- Carlyle Marney had just taught me what being *Priests to Each Other* was really all about.

Wow!

(More on Vietnam in following chapter)

Chapter 9

In His Steps

> "A brave man struggling in the storms of fate,
> and greatly falling with a falling state."
> Alexander Pope

"Freeeeze!" was the shouted command to the small platoon. They were crossing a land mine implanted field in the Vietnam Delta. The reason for the command was that one young soldier had just become a casualty. He had stepped on a land mine, and the explosion had ripped off his legs, and through his torso. He lay dying in a mass of torn flesh and blood.

The freeze command was to prevent someone else from having the same demise. Until those with the mine detectors cleared the area for medics, everyone else was to stand completely frozen in their tracks. ·That's what haunted Bob the most.

Looking over his shoulder, Bob realized that the latest victim of the Vietnam war was the man immediately behind him just five paces back. Walking single file, this dying comrade had done what all the others were doing, stepped in the footprints of the man in front. Bob's friend lay dying after having stepped in a footprint he had just left. Only a fraction of an inch could have separated life from death.   Ten years later, he was still having nightmares about that horror, and numerous others from his time in Southeast Asia.

Bob was a veteran beat cop who worked the streets. He was a good policeman. Strong, fit, level-headed, articulate, and smart. He came for therapy because of the recurring nightmares and his overreaction to certain situations that occurred in the line of duty.

When he was called on to intervene in a situation that involved an Asian, male or female, that looked ever so faintly like a Vietnamese, he would feel enormous rage inside. He never lost control, but was terrified he might.

Bob was suffering from Post Traumatic Stress Disorder, better known as PTSD. That's a diagnosis that was devised by the American Psychiatric Association for veterans of the Vietnam war. So many of them had post-war problems, that a whole new category of emotional disorder was defined to label this condition. It has since been broadened to include other experiences, but the original usage of PTSD was limited to Vietnam veterans.

Bob's particular version of trauma included a heavy

dose of *survivor's syndrome.* He felt intense guilt and shame at being spared when his friend had died stepping in the tracks he had just left. His feelings were not rational, but they were real, and they had converted to generalized depression that got worse and worse.

During his individual therapy sessions, Bob would talk quietly about his life and the war. But, he had almost no affect; his emotions were flat-lined. He wasn't sad, hurt, angry, or afraid. Neither was he happy, contented, or peaceful. He was shut down.

When your emotional system shuts down, it knocks out both sides of the signal-- no pleasure and no pain. The emotional defense system isn't capable of filtering out bad feelings while allowing good feelings to pass through. No, when your defense system comes to the rescue, it blocks out all the juices. Thus, it had for Bob.

When this happens, feelings go underground and began to subconsciously control your life. It's common to hear someone say, "I keep my feelings to myself. I don't let my feelings show."

Unfortunately, that isn't true. Feelings don't ever stay inside. In some form or fashion, they come out. Like an old car with an oil leak, one way or the other, it'll mess up the garage floor. Thus it is with feelings that are held inside. One way or the other, feelings that are undealt with and unresolved will leak out in the form of depression, anxiety, compulsivity, headaches, stomach aches, "acting out" or a dozen other ways. But they do come out.

QUESTION. *What is the tipoff that such is happening?*

ANSWER. *When your actions are markedly different than your convictions or beliefs.* The wider the gap between actions and convictions, the more your life is being controlled by unresolved feelings.

People who are well integrated are clearly congruent in Thinking, Feeling, and Acting. The following graphic illustrates my idea of a well-integrated life. It shows thinking, feeling, acting as closely connected, though not perfectly overlapping. I believe getting to the place when *what we think, how we feel,* and *how we act* are completely the same is reserved for "the great not yet."

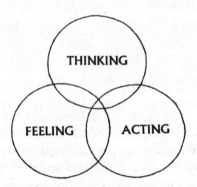

Due to his PTSD, Bob's Thinking, Feeling, and Acting were miles apart. To change that, he desperately needed some healing from some deep emotional wounds.

After a substantial amount of individual therapy, I persuaded Bob to join my weekly therapy group. He agreed, "Provided I don't have to say anything." Assuming he would eventually open up, I assured him that would work. Little did I know he meant it.

For the first six weeks, Bob scarcely said a word. Occasionally, he would ask someone to clarify something that was said. But he never volunteered anything about himself. Nor would he answer directly if someone asked him a question.

However, over a period of time, slowly but surely, he began to open up. He told his story, felt his feelings, and got better. After several months, he became a vital part of that group experience. He even took our Group Leadership Training course for laity and para-professionals. He stayed in my group for a few years, and his growth continued to amaze me. Perhaps the following story tells it best.

After two fellow police officers were killed in the line of duty, Bob wrote a piece that was distributed throughout the department. It was unsigned.

****

With love, ...a fellow Beat Cop

Sometimes being a police officer hurts. Today is precisely one of those times. The emotional pain is intense. Without warning, two friends have been cruelly severed from our midst. Forever, they are gone. Despite our prayers, there will be no return.

Noone was prepared for their senseless departure.The bloodied transgression will never be explained. Co-workers and loved ones didn't even have a chance to say goodbye. Those of us left behind will continue to face the pretensions of everyday life. In our mourning, tender hearts are fully exposed. Confusion bonds itself to our own mortality. We are vulnerable in our vengeance, fear, and love.

During our grief, strangers will pry. A quest to answer the answerable begins. The news media, representing a bereaving and curious community, will unintentionally exploit insignificant innuendos prior to the conclusions of comprehensive internal and external investigations. Citizens will momentarily ponder. A grand jury will digest clinical facts in a comfortable courtroom.

Professionals, both renowned and self-appointed, will analyze and dissect a senseless tragedy. Police training films will be produced in a valiant effort to prevent reoccurrences. Reams of paper will record and document the thunder which occurred over a period of but a few minutes. But through it all, the Police Department begins reflecting upon its deep inner loss. Two fallen comrades are dead. Remaining behind are the unanswerable questions, personal reflections, camaraderie, memories.

Dealing with the pretensions and neuroses of an often confusing world, along with the sometimes silly internal hassles, is a nuisance endured within our Department family. Every now and then, reality strikes an excruciating blow. The stressful nuisances of everyday life are set aside. Flickering priorities are rekindled.

In the aftermath of Black Friday's tragedy, grief and shock prevent the expression of our innermost feelings. Tears may mask the pain, but absolutely nothing can hide the helplessness. The sheer rage will have to be buried. Perhaps, the repressed feelings will be called upon to provide inner strength that will be necessary for future perils.

Regardless of the pecking order-- from the Chief to the most recently hired police recruit-- we are now temporarily equal. Extreme feelings force unity. Pain, sorrow, anger, and compassion reach into the very depths of our souls. The sleepless nights begin.

Our awakened values are reaffirmed. With God's help, those values will remain intact. Our stars will shine as we prepare for a return to the pretensions of everyday life. The death of our friends will contribute to the significance of our own personal journeys. Somehow, the troubled paths may even be less difficult.

Thank you, Lord, for allowing me to be part of the Department Family. For without that, I would never have known these two fine men. My life is now entrusted in preserving them exactly as they were: Two good street cops and two good friends.

May they rest in peace. The cherished memories shall help protect those who remain.

With love,

... a fellow Beat Cop

As you now understand, Bob is a most remarkable man. He's one of my heroes. He also serves as a reminder to me of the horrific effect of the Vietnam war on this country and on me personally. Let me explain.

In the summer of 1963, I graduated from college, got married, and joined the Navy. The war in Southeast Asia was escalating at a hot and heavy pace. Military recruiters were permanent fixtures in the student centers on college campuses. I was not a gung ho military guy. However, being an officer was more appealing to me than being drafted into the Army. So, rather than be drafted, I signed up for an officer program.

My choice of naval aviation did not come from a burning desire to fly an airplane or earn those *Navy Wings of Gold.* I chose Naval Aviation Officer Candidate School because I liked the idea of training in Pensacola, Florida, rather than Quantico, Virginia; San Antonio, Texas; or Newport, Rhode Island. That may not be the best reason to pick a billet or branch of the service, but it seemed like the thing to do at the time.

During the war, I spent three years as a Naval Aviation Officer (1963-66.) In that period of time, I had several friends and classmates from the training command who were killed. Some were POW's. Some for a long time. In my case, without rhyme or reason, all of my assignments were in the States. Due to the luck of the draw, I spent my entire military career in Florida.

While I was raising a family and living safely on American soil, numerous others were dying a senseless death or rotting away in a prison camp. I experienced numerous internal conflicts about that. Examples:

(1) Although I came to strongly oppose the war, I deeply supported the military men and women.

(2) I supported the war protestors who were marching against the political charade, but I resented the protestors who directed their attacks at the military personnel who were fighting the war.

(3) I had no problem with celebrities like Jane Fonda speaking against the war, but I hated her posing in Hanoi with those who were killing American G.I.'s.

(4) I was sympathetic to the conscientious objectors who fled to Canada, but I also defended those who volunteered for Vietnam duty.

Do you get the picture? Along with countless others, for me, it was a time of enormous contradictions and conflicts. My internal battle was compounded by a strange sense of irrational shame. The fickle finger of fate had given me a cushy ride; my friends were not so lucky.

Maybe that's why I've always felt such a connection when I've done therapy with Vietnam vets. In some strange, unconscious, irrational way, maybe it feels like I'm making up for the lucky break that I didn't deserve.

Maybe that's why I felt so connected to Bob. Here is a man who walked across a mine field one day and didn't get a scratch. The guy behind him stepped in his foot prints and was blown into Eternity.

Just writing this makes me aware that I need to probe and process this issue some more. Probably ought to spend some time in Purgatory Cove at DFCC. Yeah, I think I'd better purge that some more. I'm sure of it.

Chapter 10

Nolo Contendere

> "When marriage is a contest,
> there are no winners."
> Author

lazy
drinks too much
watches TV too much
doesn't listen...

She was fifteen minutes late for her first session. As I walked out to look for her in the office complex lobby, I thought she might be having trouble finding my suite. Since we had only spoken by phone, I didn't know what she looked like, but I remembered how hyper she sounded. When I spotted a woman moving like she was *on a mission,* I asked her if she was looking for my office.

With a scowl on her face and an edge in her voice, she exclaimed, "Yessss!" She began talking.

She was late because I had given poor directions. She didn't have time to waste, and she had a lot to tell. She expected me to make up the lost time because of my poor directions. She wanted her money's worth from her two-hour session. (All of this was said as we walked down the hallway.)

Entering the office, I asked if she wanted something to drink. She declined, saying she didn't want to waste her time "fooling with something to drink."

As she continued her litany, I poured myself a cup of extra strong coffee, and I remembered the woman who said to her therapist, "If you weren't so stupid, you could tell me why nobody likes me!") By the time I sat down, she had opened her legal pad. The hunt was on.

"You want to know what's wrong with my husband? I'll tell you what's wrong with my husband. I don't know what he told you. But I'm going to set the record straight." (I had seen him the week before.)

For the next full hour, she read her list and expounded on each one. The best I could count, she had sixty-three complaints and criticisms of her husband of nine years.

Three times during that hour, I attempted to interact with her and get her more productively focused. However, she wasn't finished with her list, and was not going to be distracted.

Finally, much to my surprise, she said, "So, what do you think about that? Huh? Huh?"

I responded quickly, lest she change her mind. Smiling, I said, "Why've you stay married to a man with that many faults? Have you thought of killing him? With that much wrong with him, he doesn't deserve to live!"

"Well, he's not **that** bad," she said, with a smile.

Afraid she was going to get the floor again, I quickly

continued, "Well, let me be totally serious with you. This marriage doesn't have a chance unless you're willing to trade in your microscope for a mirror."

While this story represents the extreme, many couples suffer from the same *mortal marital malady*: THE CONTEST-- a pathological state of competition.

"You're wrong."

"You're to blame."

"You did it."

"It's your fault."

"The trouble with you is..."

"You always..."

"You never..."

It's a constant contest of blame, criticism, control. When I talk with couples locked up in THE CONTEST, I'm reminded of the song that said, "That's when two fools collide."

To revive a struggling marriage, you must see the relationship as the third party in the pyramid-- **you, me, and we.** And the WE portion is barely alive in ICU; perhaps on life-support systems.

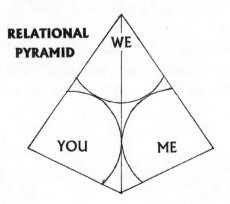

RELATIONAL PYRAMID

WE

YOU

ME

The previous graphic helps to create a clear mental image of the point I am making. **You, Me**, and **We**-- the three entities that make up an intimate relationship.

With mirror in hand, two questions are pertinent:

(1)What have I done to contribute to the illness in this relationship?

(2)What am I willing to do to help it recover?

If the answer to these questions are not clear and harmonious with both parties, then professional help is definitely required. Or the relationship is probably not going to leave ICU.

The chorus of a pop song from a few years back offers a good beginning for a struggling marriage. "There ain't no good guys. There ain't no bad guys. There's only you and me, and we just disagree."

Over the past thirty years, I've seen remarkable changes in marriages when both people get on the same side of the battle line. *I've seldom seen any substantial change unless they do*. Some couples stay together for years with their relationship (the third party) in intensive care. It never revives and never functions. It just stays barely alive by artificial means.

You've taken a giant step toward resolution when you finally say:

"Nolo contendere. The contest is over. Hand me the mirror. Our relationship has a problem. What have I done to contribute to the malady? What can I do to help it recover?"

Chapter 11

A Field of Shattered Dreams

> "What happens to a shattered dream?
> Does it dry up like a raisin in the sun,
> Or fester like a sore and run?"
> Langston Hughes

Landon dreamed daily of playing major league baseball. Stan Musical, Enos Slaughter, Marty Marion, and Terry Moore were his heroes. Yes, he would play for the St. Louis Cardinals.

At age fifteen, coaches were saying he was sure to make it. He could hit for average, and with power. His arm was like a cannon. And he could run. He also had the heart. He practiced harder than the others, and talked the game from daylight to dark.

Other boys wanted it; Landon had the passion for it. His motto was: "Determination rather than desire controls your destiny!" He would make it to the majors. Then, he got polio. Horrors. His left leg withered.

The church prayed. The minister prophesied that God would heal Landon. They had prayer meetings, laid on hands, and poured on holy oil. He believed. Polio was just a temporary setback. He dreamed he would be back on the field in no time. He would show them. He would give the glory to God. He would become a preacher, and a major league baseball player.

Around the country, he would give speeches to youth about God, faith, and perseverance. He would be an inspiration to the masses. Landon would be a model Christian citizen who had overcome polio, who was a minister of the gospel, and played for the Cardinals.

His bargaining didn't work. Neither did the prayers, the prophesying, nor the anointing with oil. It didn't happen. He never recovered. He never really played ball again. Oh, he tried, but his bad leg eliminated any possibility of excelling in baseball.

For all of Landon's adult life, that withered leg was an unconscious reminder of a shattered dream. Losing his dream, he lost hope. Without hope, he gave up his faith. In the absence of hope and faith, there was very little capacity to love and be loved. That's a principle that needs to be repeated: *When a person is without hope or faith, the ability to love is greatly impaired.*

In Landon's case, without hope and faith, all that was left was a man who was cantankerous, compulsive, angry, and almost devoid of any sense of humor.

Landon's lack of humor was a sharp contrast to a man I once knew. My friend was faced with heart bypass surgery (when that procedure was in its infancy stage.) The night before the operation, the surgeon gave a somber report about the dangers, warnings, and risks.

My friend asked, "Doc, if I survive this heart surgery, will I be able to play the trumpet?"

"Of course, you will," the doctor said reassuringly. "After you get over the soreness and get your strength back, you can certainly play the trumpet."

"That'll be a consolation, and a miracle," said my friend. "I've never played the trumpet in my life."

Landon didn't have such a sense of humor. He was the victim of a horrible illness. He was then victimized by religious fanatics who *promised what they couldn't deliver.* The latter was more devastating than the former. As a result, he found nothing in life to laugh about.

Forty years after his illness, Landon came for intensive therapy. He was surprised when I proposed we talk in depth about his polio. Over the years, he had seen numerous therapists. But he had never told the painful story of his withered leg. What surfaced was staggering. For hours on end, he sobbed about his shattered dream.

One homework assignment included watching the movie, "Field of Dreams." It's a great picture about broken dreams and baseball. Landon couldn't stop watching it. It was *his* story; *his* life; *his* unhealed shattered dream.

Well, what do you do with your shattered dreams? How do you handle the loss of your hopes and aspirations? Do you grieve normally, expressing your feelings in a healthy way? Do you suppress your feelings? Live in denial? Get stuck in bitterness and anger, as did Landon?

A few years ago, a personal loss in my life left me with deep sadness. I cried many tears and felt deep pain. Then the tears dried up. I was left with anger and bitterness. The slightest memory of the loss would set me off in a cycle of obsessing. Mostly feeling hostility at those who had caused it, my shattered dream, though minor in contrast to many others, was tormenting.

How about you? Have you had to deal with a shattered dream? Did you grieve it normally and healthily? Or bury it? Or deny it?

"Les Miserables" is one of the longest running Broadway musicals of all time. Toward the end of the play, after the revolution has failed, one of the survivors sings the powerful "Empty Chairs at Empty Tables."

****

> There's a grief that can't be spoken
> There's a pain goes on and on
> Empty chairs at empty tables
> Now my friends are dead and gone.
> Here they talked of revolution
> Here it was they lit the flame
> Here they sang about tomorrow
> And tomorrow never came.

****

Shattered dreams are a part of life. Everyone's life. In fact, a large portion of those who come for therapy are back packing a broken dream. Sometimes it's a repressed broken dream that is hidden away in the unconscious mind, and the event itself is below the memory level.

More often the event is clearly retrievable, but the *feelings* related to the event are totally repressed.

In my experience, the latter is much more damaging than the former. Therapeutically, I'm more concerned about dredging up repressed feelings than repressed events.

Years ago, Jean, a chronically depressed, middle-aged, woman came for therapy. After much probing and little results, I finally found what Dr. Cecil Osborne called "the black cat in the dark room."

When Jean was thirteen, her only brother was killed in WW II. When she told that story, she remembered no details and had no emotion whatsoever. Recalling her brother's death produced no more affect than telling me what she had for dinner. When I asked for detailed memories about the tragedy-- the funeral, reaction of family members, and particularly what she remembered feeling at the time-- she drew a blank.

Then she said, "I do have one clear memory about Bubbie's death."

When I asked her to relive it to release it, she starred off in the distance and said, " I can still see the picture in the newspaper and the caption on the clipping. It was at the train depot. There was a casket with an American flag over it. And the caption read, 'Local Soldier Finally Comes Home.' That's all I can remember."

"That's enough," I said.

With some persistent intensive work, using that one event-memory, we unearthed an emotional mine shaft of feeling-memory and relieved a life-time of mild to moderate depression.

Yes, sooner or later, shattered dreams are a part of nearly everyone's life. How we handle them controls our peace of mind.

After far too many years of misery, Landon finally unwound his ball of twine, and truly began his journey toward wholeness. It was a remarkable experience.

In all my years of doing therapy, I've never had anyone work any harder with anymore determination than Landon. For the first time since polio shattered his dream, he retrieved his competitive edge and applied that motivation to heal his internal wounds.

Similar to Jean, regarding her brother's death, Landon had buried the feeling-memory. Unlike Jean, as evidenced by his crippled leg, his event-memory was a constant companion. But Landon paid the price, did the work, and worked his program, and his life changed dramatically.

In his own words, "The intensive work I did at DFCC was the beginning step of my new life. How thankful I am that I had that good fortunate. . . I will be forever grateful."

So will we, Landon. So will we.

Chapter 12

"Is Yore Name Boyles?"

> "Some of my cherished experiences
> have come from the most unlikely
> people and places."   Author

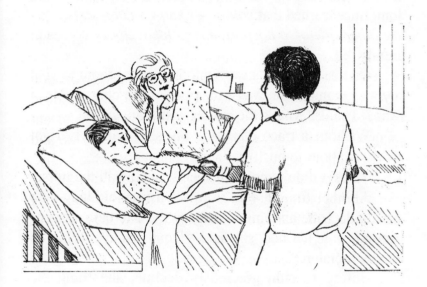

Semi-private rooms made up the south wing of
Clinch Memorial Hospital. Patients on this wing were
those on Medicare or Medicaid. Most of them had fixed
incomes, and poor insurance coverage.

By contrast, the north wing at CMH had private
rooms for patients who were economically sound or had
generous insurance coverage. Or both.

As pastor of a small county seat *First Church*, my

time in making hospital visits was quite equally divided between the two wings; just as our church was pretty equally divided between the *haves* and the *have nots*.

Room 103 was on the semi-private south wing and was my first pastoral stop of the day. I was there for a visit with a lady who was a member of my flock. It was a routine I had repeated hundreds of times. Little did I know, this visit would be different. As a pastor, I had long since learned that *you never know what to expect on the other side of a hospital door.* One memory comes to mind.

On one occasion, I went into a hospital room to visit a young woman who was a member of our church. "Jean Ann," I said, "what's the matter with you, girl?"

Without a trace of inhibition, she said, "My right ovary is about to bust."

Yikes! I didn't know whether to run or call the nurse!

Another time, I went in to see a very old lady who had undergone abdominal surgery the day before. As I stood beside her bed, she said, "Don, would you like to see by incision?"

Before I could graciously decline, she flung the covers back and showed me much more than I was interesting in seeing. A whole lot more. At that moment, I was terrified she was going to ask for a "laying on of hands!"

So, although hospital visits often brought unexpected experiences, the story I'm about to tell was extraordinary. In fact, it wins the ribbon as the most surprising hospital visit I ever experienced.

Entering the room, I said, "Good morning" to my

parishioner who was in the first bed. Looking toward the other bed, I smiled, nodded politely, and said "Hello" to a woman whom I did not know, and to my knowledge, had never before seen.

Walking up to the bedside of the one I had come to visit, I shook her hand, and asked how she was feeling. Her response was interrupted by the lady in the far bed.

"You-a-preacha?" she asked, as if it was all one word.

As I looked around, she was rolling up on her elbow, and folding a pillow up under her head.

Smiling, I responded, "Sometimes."

"I meant, ain't-chew-a reverent?"

"Sometimes," I countered, still smiling.

"Don't-chew-preach at that big church down on the highway?" she persisted.

"Sometimes," I persisted, also.

"Ain't yore name Boyles?" she continued, nodding her head as if she knew the answer.

"Well, that's close enough," I said.

"I knowed who you was when you walked in yhere. Knowed it was you when I first laid eyes on you. Mr. Jack said you look like a bulldog, and you do."

Moving toward the lady with all the questions, I said to my church member, "Excuse me, I'll be right back."

As I approached the other bed, I stuck out my hand and said, "You seem to know a lot more about me than I do about you. Who might you be?"

"Name's Minnie Miller," she said. "I live on Mr. Jack's egg farm. Used to go to yore church. But I stopped going sixteen-year ago."

"Why did you stop?" I asked.

"They hurt my feelings in that Sunday School class."

"If it kept you from going for that long, it must have been pretty bad," I said sympathetically. "What did they do to you?"

"Don't remember," she said. "Been so long, I done slap forgot. Here lately, I'd been studying about coming back. But, then you hurt my feelings again when you stopped sending me them papers."

I was hard pressed to keep a straight face, and at a loss over "them papers." Then it hit me.

"Do you mean the church newsletter that goes out periodically, the one called *The Belfrey?*"

"That's hit," she said.

Taking out a pencil and small note pad, I said, "If you will give me your address, I'll personally see to it that you start getting the church paper again. And I hope you'll give us another chance, and come back to church when you get to feeling better."

I shook her hand and walked back to the other bed to resume my visit with the lady I'd come to visit. After a few minutes, I said a prayer for both women and left.

Two Sundays later, after the morning worship service, I was standing at the door greeting people as they were leaving the sanctuary. A strange little lady with a noticeable limp waddled up and stuck out her hand.

Not recognizing her, I said, "How're you this morning? Glad to see you. I don't believe I know you."

With unbridled irritation, she said, "Don't know me? Why, I'm Minnie Miller! You done seen me in the hospital two weeks ago!"

"Oh God," I thought, "there goes another sixteen years!"

Gasping for breath, I was desperate for a way to get out of this predicament. And at that very moment, without question, I experienced an instant of divine intervention. I haven't had many of those in my life. (Some folks in our church were convinced I'd never had any moments of divine intervention.) But at that moment, Moses and the burning bush had nothing on me. No doubt about it, Almighty God himself, or herself, intervened on my behalf.

Flashing a big flirtatiously teasing smile, I said, "Why Miss Minnie, of course, that's you. I nearly didn't recognize you **with your clothes on!**"

She cackled with laughter, punched me on the shoulder, and said, "Aw Boyles, get on away from yheah. You a mess Boyles-- don't-chew-know?"

Under my breath, I sighed, "Thank you, Lord. God, I thank you." Later that day, the saga continued.

Our Sunday evening service was at seven o'clock. Around six o'clock, the phone rang at my house and the voice said, "Boyles, this yeah is Minnie Miller. I was planning on coming to church tonight."

"That's fine, Miss Minnie, I'm glad to hear it. I'll look forward to seeing you."

"Problem is-- I don't have a ride. Reckon you could come get me?"

"Well, of course I can," I said, not sure what I was getting into. "Where do you live?" Afraid to hear the answer, I was concerned she might be like some of our folks who lived so far back in the woods they had to *walk toward town to hunt.* I was holding my breath that she wasn't one of them.

"On Mr. Jack's egg farm, just like I told you, Boyles. Tain't far."

Still hoping she was shooting straight about the distance, I pleaded: "Well, would you be kind enough to give me a hint in which direction, and on what street?"

She finally told me. And I finally found her. It was only about a mile to her house. After the evening service, I returned her to her home.

The work week came and so did Mid-Week Prayer Meeting. The call came to the house.

"Boyles, I was hoping to come to prayer meeting."

"I'll be there Miss Minnie."

During the Sunday School hour, of the following Sunday morning, I was in my study at the church. The phone rang three or four times. Since no one answered out in the office, I picked it up in my study.

"Church office," I said.

"Boyles? I been a waitin' on you to get me for Sunday School. You're already late, and you're about to hurt my feelings. Now see yheah, if I can't depend on you, I'll find me another church."

"Miss Minnie, give me one more chance. I'll be there before you can get your coat on."

That routine continued for several weeks. Various people volunteered to help me transport her. I resisted. Minnie Miller was one of the most interesting people I had ever met. I wasn't about to give up that time together. I suspected that behind all that gruffness, harshness, and anger was a woman with a lot of heartache and pain in her life. I was right. I asked her questions, listened to her, teased and kidded with her, and told her jokes.

Frequently she would say, "Boyles, you a mess, don't-chew-know?"

After we built enough trust, she began to tell her story. Back and forth between her house and the church, she unfolded her life, chapter by chapter, verse by verse. What a story! One that will be saved for another time.

One Sunday evening, just as I was beginning my sermon, she had a seizure. We called for the ambulance, and called off the service. While they took her to the hospital, I went to get her husband.

As I went into her room at the hospital, she said, "Boyles, sorry about ruining yore sermon."

"Miss Minnie," I said, "you did me a favor, I didn't have much of a sermon anyway."

"Boyles," she said, "you a mess, don't-chew-know?"

After several months, I finally yielded to a request from the deacons that they would at least take over transporting her on Sunday mornings, and other times when I needed them. I checked it out with Miss Minnie. She wasn't too pleased, but assured me she wouldn't quit for another sixteen years.

After ten years as a pastor in Homerville, Georgia, in 1979, we moved to Burlingame, California. We took with us a lifetime of memories from that decade in South Georgia. Certainly, in the top ten list of special memories was of one, Minnie Miller.

Two years later, we came back for a visit. The pastor asked me to preach during morning worship. At the close of the service, he asked me to go to the back of the church so people could come by to say "hello."

As heads were bowed and the benediction was being said, I was walking down the aisle. About a third of the way out, I heard, "Pssstt, pssstt." I stopped and looked around. You guessed it.

"Boyles," she said, "you still a mess, don't-chew-know?"

"You're right, Miss Minnie, and so are you."

As I continued walking down the aisle, I was thinking how the Minnie Millers of the world have blessed my life. They're the down-and-outers who come across as rude and harsh, but underneath are just suffering souls with the same needs as everyone else. They're starving to be loved and cared for, and when they are, they will give back far more than you have given them.

As my eyes began to water, I cleared my throat and whispered under my breath:

"Thank you, Lord, for Minnie Miller, and for teaching me that you never know what you're going to find on the other side of a hospital door. Don't-chew-know?"

Chapter 13

Nervous BreakTHROUGH

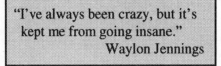

"I've always been crazy, but it's
kept me from going insane."
Waylon Jennings

She had shared a lot of facts that were devoid of
feelings. The longer she talked, the less she said.

Interrupting her, I said, "Will you let yourself **feel**
what you are saying?"

With grave concern, she retorted, "Feel what I am
saying? If I start crying, I'm afraid I'll never stop. If I get
angry, I might go berserk. If I let my feelings out, I could

go insane."

The truth is-- *no one ever went insane from letting their feelings out. Many have gone insane from holding their feelings in.*

Sandra's story illustrates my point. When she called DFCC to make an appointment, she sounded desperate. Although my schedule was quite full, I agreed to see her late in the afternoon.

When she began talking, she thanked me for seeing her on such short notice, and she apologized for making my day longer. Assuring her it was okay, I asked her to tell me what had prompted her call.

In a very soft and tiny voice, Sandra said she was frightened about her recent irrational thoughts and actions. Sometimes, while driving down the freeway, she would have an urge to drive excessively fast. At times, she would envision driving her car into a bridge abutment at a high rate of speed. The worst part was that she would have these urges even when her baby girl was in the car.

As she shared this information, she leaked a few tears, but never made any noise. When I asked her what was going on in her life that was making her angry, she indicated nothing. Then, I asked her to tell me her current life story. It was a little bizarre.

Sandra was in her mid-twenties, and had been married to Larry for three years. She was a legal secretary. Larry was unemployed. It seemed he never had been able to keep a job; she had been the primary bread winner from the *get-go*. As she filled in the blanks, the picture began to clear up.

For about a year, a woman named Joyce had been

living with them. Larry had met Joyce in a bar. According to Sandra, they were "just friends."

Continuing her story, she said Larry never helped with the housework, and gave only a minimum of attention to the baby. Joyce didn't have a job either, and did no chores around the house.

Sandra worked all day, picked up the baby from daycare, made dinner when she got home, bathed the baby, put her to bed, cleaned up the kitchen, and straightened the house. Larry and Joyce watched television, laughed, and horsed around while Sandra was attending to all of the aforementioned responsibilities.

After Sandra would go to bed, Larry and Joyce would sometimes go out bar hopping, and come back quite late. Sometimes, Larry would join Sandra in bed; sometimes not. Her explanation? "He and Joyce both have insomnia, so they just stay up together."

How convenient, I thought. They sleep all day while Sandra's at work, and then stay up all night while she's asleep. Listening to Sandra tell this story, I was shocked at the lack of emotion in her voice.

For sure, I was not totally objective when I asked, "Don't you think they're fooling around?"

"Oh, no. I asked Larry. He told me they weren't," she said with assurance.

So, I took another approach. "Aren't you angry at the way you're being treated?"

"Oh, no. The Bible talks against anger. I don't believe in getting mad. It's not the way I was raised. Besides, Mama says people who get angry sometimes go crazy."

Seeing that she was in real trouble and I was running out of time, I went for the jugular. For the next ten minutes, I recounted and rephrased what she had been telling me. For emphasis, I went to the *Don Doyle A-material for special effects.* Actually, I embellished and dramatized it is what I did. I was determined to get the lid off this young woman's rage.

The justification for my aggressive approach was quite simple. She was so out of touch with her feelings, she was thinking of killing herself and her baby by driving into a bridge abutment! She was blaming and shaming herself for having such feelings. But the only thing that was wrong with this young woman's present life was a worthless piece of garbage named Larry, and his trashy bimbo named Joyce. I didn't have much time to get this woman's aggression focused in the right direction. So, I milked it for all it was worth.

Finishing, I said, "Having heard me TRANSLATE what you have told me, what do you FEEL like doing?"

Her face strained and began to turn red. Her breathing became short, fast, and audible. She still didn't speak for nearly a minute.

I goaded her on. "What do you feel like doing?" I asked, motioning with my hand as if to pull the feelings out of her body.

With that she jumped up, surged her hands high and yelled, "I'd like to kill that s.o.b.!" She ran across the room, pounded a table with both fists. Then she yelled to the top of her petite lungs, "I'd really like to kill that worthless _____ and that _____ he's _____."

As if she were delivering a monologue, she

continued for at least fifteen minutes. Part of what she half-whispered under her breath included: "You've treated me like a piece of garbage; you stupid ____ ! Well, you and your little bar room cutie are in for a big surprise!"

Epilogue. You'll be interested to know that when Sandra got home, she encouraged Larry and Joyce to go to a movie. While they were gone, she called a locksmith who changed the locks. Then she put all their clothes out in the yard, took her baby, and left town for the weekend.

It wasn't the end of her therapy, but I'd say it was a pretty good beginning. I'd also say that Sandra got her money's worth out of one two-hour therapy session.

****

Moral. Like Sandra, numerous people in our culture have been programmed into holding their feelings in for fear they will go crazy or have a nervous breakdown. In Sandra's case, as with countless others, **she was about to have a breakdown from holding all those feelings inside.**

Quite often in therapy, when feelings start coming out, I give assurance they are having a *nervous breakTHROUGH*, not a nervous breakdown.

Due in large measure to this erroneous perception, lots of people have victimized themselves physically, mentally, emotionally, and spiritually by repressing and suppressing their feelings.

To be sure, there are inappropriate ways to express feelings. I'm not suggesting it is healthy to carry our feelings on our sleeves, nor constantly unload them on those around us.

What I am proposing is that we start telling ourselves the truth-- *feelings are just feelings.* There's no value judgment placed on them. Feelings are not right or wrong, good or bad. Feelings are not normal or abnormal, moral or immoral. (You can't have an immoral feeling).

Feelings just are... well, feelings; that's what they are... nothing more, nothing less. And they're a big part of what it means to be human. Feelings are just feelings; until you do something with them, they can't be critiqued.

Holding feelings in will make you sick, and that's unhealthy. Dumping them inappropriately on others is destructive, and that's unacceptable. *But having feelings, all feelings, and being honest about them, and taking the responsibility for appropriately expressing them is a step toward wholeness.*

Of all feelings, **anger** is the most mishandled because it's usually dealt with by holding it in or by blasting others. Both of these choices are destructive.

The healthy way to deal with anger is to express it using **I** messages. "**I** feel angry," rather than, "**You're** such a witch!" "**I** feel resentment over cleaning up after you," rather than, "**You** never do anything around here!"

No doubt, *expressing anger* rather than using an *angry expression* is much more palatable to all of us, and enhances emotional intimacy in all relationships.

So, the next time you feel angry or feel like crying, let it happen. Tell yourself the truth. In so doing, you're *Going Sane,* rather than insane. You're having a nervous breakTHROUGH, rather than a nervous breakdown.

Chapter 14

"Yippy Ki Yea..."

> "All the happy people I know are people I don't know very well."
> Dennis Prager

As the garage door came up, Sam was surprised that Susan's Oldsmobile Bravada was not in its place. It was 9:30 p.m. on Sunday evening, not a normal time for Susan to be out of the house.

Sam had been on a four-day golfing trip to Hilton Head, South Carolina. Unloading his bags from the Cadillac, he opened the door to their palatial home with marble columns which overlooked the city of Cincinnati. What he saw was a sight he will never forget. It was not the night lights of the city. The house was empty!

Instantly, he thought robbery. Rushing through the house, he noticed everything was gone except his own personal items. That's when his fear turned to his worst nightmare. There was no robbery. His wife Susan had left him and taken everything with her. It's a fair assessment to say, *she had taken the gold mine and given him the shaft.*

Telling me the story, he said, "All she left me was a plastic utensil set from Kentucky Fried Chicken."

Even though that mental imagery struck me as hilarious, somehow I managed not to laugh.

Sam's mind immediately went back to the Wednesday night before he left for Hilton Head. An argument between them got out of control. He'd said some very ugly and nasty things to Susan. He remembered how mad he was, and how hurt and upset she was. Remembering that he had left early on Thursday morning without even saying goodbye, he began to hyperventilate.

Later that evening, he discovered a note that read: "Enough is enough. Don't try to find me. You can't. Don't think I'm bluffing. I'm not. I've accepted a job in Atlanta. I'm outta here. Yippy Ki Yea, _____ _____!"

That's when his hyperventilating got worse. That's when he fell on his knees on the plush deep-pile carpet in the totally empty bedroom. For the first time in years, he sobbed, and sobbed, and sobbed.

Sam knew a psychotherapist in Cincinnati, and called her. Knowing Sam, and having referred about a dozen people to us, she was also quite familiar with our intensive program. She referred him to DFCC. Within twenty-four hours Sam called me. That's when the healing began.

Now, let's rewind this tape and get to know Sam and Susan. What was so wrong with this marriage that brought on this radical departure? We'll start with Sam.

Sam was an extremely angry man who kept it under control with everyone except his wife. In almost all relationships, except the most important one, he was Mr. Nice Guy. He was likeable and lovable. He told great jokes. He entertained; the life of the party. But not with Susan, nor his two previous wives. With them, it was all too common for him to be quick tempered, hostile, and verbally abusive. Incidently, both his other marriages had ended with both women leaving him, just not so dramatically as Susan.

Sam was typical of a large segment of the male populace whose *emotion of choice is anger.* Along with many others, that's the only way he knew how to express his feelings-- through the emotion of anger. When he was hurt, he showed anger. When he was fearful, he expressed anger. When he was frustrated, irritated, or disappointed, he displayed anger. When he felt guilt, he emoted anger. He was an angry man who was trying to empty a bathtub with an eye dropper. That's a tough job.

Susan, on the other hand, was passive-aggressive. She almost never expressed or demonstrated any feelings. Instead, when faced with feelings (especially anger) being expressed by a man, she withdrew. She retreated. A case could be made to say she pouted. However, I'll give her a break and call it withdrawal. When Sam was angry, she *suppressed* her feelings, and went into her shell. She took numerous, lengthy, hot baths. For hours at a time, she went hiking-- alone. She had done this with her two previous husbands, also. In fact, she had done this with every man in her life, which is a story we'll get to later.

But lo and behold, one day, her bucket of repressed feelings got full. That's when she did the ultimate act of passive aggression-- she packed her bags, and a moving van, and left.

Now we pick up the story where Sam schedules an *Intensive Relational Integration Therapy* session for himself. In our program, that means doing thirty hours of therapy in five days.*

On the phone, he said, "This is the third wife that's left me. I don't want a third divorce. I'm ready to stop blaming them. I want to honestly look at myself."

"Good move, Sam," I said. "I don't know if we can save your marriage, but with that attitude, I believe we can save you. And who knows, we might salvage your marriage as well."

During his intensive, for the first time in his life, Sam opened the door to his personal history. Both his parents were alcoholic. His father physically abused him. His mother did not protect him. He hated her more than his father. When he was ten, and his brother was fourteen, they were abandoned by both parents. They survived on the streets of Philadelphia by stealing food from markets by day and robbing pay telephones at night.

In a ramshackle boarding house, Sam and his older

*For details about our program, see pages 163-170.

brother lived in one room. The house was run by an old lady who cut them some slack. She wasn't kind, but she was tolerant.

In this very tough racially mixed neighborhood of inner city Philadelphia, Sam met Father Michael, a wonderful Catholic priest. For a brief time, he attended mass. Telling that part of the story, Sam said the church was known as "Our Lady of Courageous Caucasians!"

Father Michael showered Sam with time and attention, and gave him some responsibilities as an altar boy. And taught him to love music. Even though he couldn't offset all the emotional damage that had been done to Sam, that priest is probably the only reason he didn't end up as a hardened criminal.

As a result of all his childhood experiences, Sam's life view was quite warped. To him, it was plain and simple-- *life was a game to be played; women were a commodity to be used.* He knew nothing of living, only surviving. As a man who had learned the secrets of how to play the game, he became a super salesman. He made money. **Lots** of money. But it never changed how he felt inside, nor how he treated the three women he married.

Whether in want or plenty, Sam operated from a victim/survivor position-- *take all you can get and don't look back, somebody might be gaining on you.* He was grossly insecure from a terrible self image though he never let it show.

With associates and friends, Sam covered his insecurity by being Mr. Hard Working Nice Guy. With his wives, he channeled all his feelings through anger. By not letting anyone get too close to his inner core, he felt safe. It also left him empty and lonely with mild to moderate, chronic depression.

Some people experience depression as a *state* which is circumstantial and based on current issues. Others experience depression as a *trait* which is a personality condition that stems from wounds that are old and deep.

Sam was the latter, but he didn't know it. In fact, he denied being chronically depressed, saying his depression was "only because Susan left me." But, his long standing history of having a short fuse and regularly spewing hostility at the women in his life defied his claim. As a result of his horrible childhood, he had inherited a depressive personality that fed all his hurt and horror through the anger hotline.

Sometimes, we forget that hurt and hate are two sides of the same coin. Behind every hurt, there is a hate; behind every hate, there is a hurt. Thus it was for Sam from Cincinnati. But he didn't stay that way.

He worked hard and took directions well. He unpacked his baggage *reliving and releasing* the hates, hurts, and horrors of his life-- pain that had been suppressed and repressed for a lifetime; heartache that had festered, oozed, and seeped out in the form of misdirected wrath. And he healed. He had a transformation. According to him, "A new Sam has been born again!" (Isn't there something in the Bible about that sort of thing? Somewhere in the Gospel of John? That's what I thought.)

So, what happened? Sam left Memphis. With Susan's permission, he went to Atlanta to spend the weekend with her. She was so moved, impressed, and awed that she made an appointment for her own intensive.

Susan's story was different. Her childhood had been much less traumatic. There was no outward abuse, just neglect and lack of nurturing. An emotionless set of parents had left her without any sense of bonding or closeness to anyone. The first person she ever really loved was her daughter, Annie, born when Susan was eighteen.

Susan had married the first guy who asked her. Unfortunately, he was a totally fanatical religious nut. She was seventeen. He was abusive-- physically, emotionally, and sexually. Susan stayed with him for a dozen years and gave birth to three children.

Finally, she left and spent the next few years as a single mother, eeking out a living, scratching and scraping to survive. Then the ultimate tragedy crashed into her life with an indescribable force. The worst tragedy that can befall a human being. Annie, her daughter, age nineteen, put a deer rifle into her mouth and blew her brains and skull all over the modest little house in midtown Cincinnati.

Not only was the daughter's life destroyed, the home was, also. Even after numerous professional cleanings, Susan finally had to sell the house. Practically gave it away, because fragments of brain tissue were still turning up in every crack and crevice of the bedroom, living room, and dining room.

Susan was thirty-seven and single at the time of the suicide. Twelve years later, when she came for intensive therapy, she had never really grieved her daughter's death. That's the main reason she withdrew in the face of conflict. She retreated to her inner shell-- the safe place in her life where no one could reach her, or hurt her. Given his volatile personality, on a regular basis, Sam pushed her "eject-into-outer-space button."

Like Sam, Susan unpacked her debris and got some healing for her suffering. She recognized that her withdrawal had not *caused* Sam's problem, but it had exacerbated it.

When Susan retreated, Sam felt abandoned, just as he did as a child when his mother left him, and did not protect him. Since he had never directed his anger at his mother, he dumped it on Susan. His core stuff and her core stuff had created a disastrous relationship. But all that changed. Yes, that's right; it all changed.

After Sam worked on his stuff, and Susan worked on her stuff, they did an intensive together. But, it was two different people who were now talking, sharing, relating, connecting, and loving.

Sam and Susan had been drawn together because of their *core strengths* which made a *synergetic relationship*-- a relationship where the sum of the togetherness is greater than the sum of the parts. However, due to their unresolved issues, they had been functioning out of their *core weaknesses* which was a *symbiotic relationship*-- a relationship that is basically parasitic which invariably produces an adversarial arrangement where the sum of the togetherness is less than the sum of the parts. A symbiotic relationship virtually has no chance for emotional intimacy.

The best illustration of symbiosis is from the world

of entomology. The termite survives on wood. In order to digest wood, a one cell organism must live IN the digestive tract of the termite. The end result is the termite can't live without the amoeba; the amoeba can't survive without the termite.

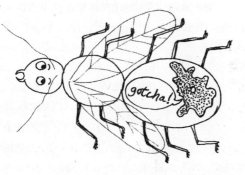

In the world of insects and lower animals, that works fine. In the arena of human relationships, it is disastrous, dysfunctional, adversarial, and doomed to miss emotional intimacy.

In the human arena, emotional intimacy comes through strengths rather than weaknesses. Yet, numerous couples have been casualties on the altar of symbiotic conflict. What drew them together was their strengths. What destroyed them was their weaknesses which were never addressed, understood, or resolved. How tragic!

Not so for Sam and Susan. After each dealt with their own pain, they did conjoint intensive therapy. We had a renewal *wedding ceremony*.

This time, they made some honest and realistic vows

to each other. We drank a toast from the fruit of the vine. They committed themselves to an experimental six-month follow-up plan which had been tailored to fit their needs.

Today, Sam and Susan are enjoying life as never before. They take long hikes *together.* He doesn't dump his anger on her. She doesn't withdraw. Frequently, he takes her to kareokee clubs and sings love songs to her with a voice that could match the best of the great crooners.

Sam and Susan still live in the marvelous house with the marble columns that overlooks Cincinnati.

Chapter 15

Bubble Boy Is Ready to Fly

> "He thought to become again the
> child he never was." The Crossing
> Cormac McCarthy

Clyde was short, frail, and walked with a limp. He was in his mid-thirties. He looked older. He had eczema all over his body; quite noticeably on his face, arms, and hands. He scratched a lot. To cope with numerous respiratory allergies, he frequently sniffed inhalers.

Clyde came for therapy to deal with his lifetime companion-- *anxiety*. Anxiety is just fear that you can't name. It feels like fear even when there's no reason for it. It's that generalized nervousness that is occasionally experienced by everyone. For masses of people, it is a constant companion. In Clyde's case, it had left him with a chronic case of mild to moderate depression. He wanted to change. I was eager to help him.

Coming for his first intensive session, which was scheduled for six straight hours, he brought a shaving kit.

Jokingly, I said, "Do you think you might need to spruce up a bit after we're finished?"

"Oh no," he replied, "this is my medicine bag." Unzipping the bag, exposing a dozen vials and sprays, he continued. "I never go anywhere without my meds. I have a set in the car, the house, and this travel kit."

"Looks like you have taken the Boy Scout motto of *Be Prepared* quite seriously," I teased.

Since he didn't laugh, I pressed on to see if he had a sense of humor. "Is that medicine bag like an American Express card, you never leave home without it?"

Seeing a slight smile, but still no laughter, I said, "Perhaps we should start your first session with you telling me the story behind *The Bag.*"

Clyde's story was strange, and very sad. Within the first few days of his birth, he was diagnosed as *extremely allergic*. He was allergic to several foods, lots of inhalants, and had numerous skin reactions. A few examples included: milk, baby powder, sunlight, pollens, polyester, sugar, eggs, cats, dogs, and humidity.

Doctors recommended a dry climate. His parents chose Phoenix. His allergies persisted. So, they moved to Las Vegas which was drier than Phoenix. (That shocked me. Folks from Phoenix think they have a lock on dry air. Bet the Chamber of Commerce would be appalled to hear someone moved from Phoenix to a *drier* climate!)

Back to Clyde. To cope with his condition, he was pampered, scolded, restricted, warned, coddled, sheltered, and *smothered by his mother.* Basically, Dad just stayed out of it, and let Mom do what she had to do. The woman had a tough job, no doubt about it, but she overdid it.

As a result of all this smothering, Clyde was a social misfit. He was so self-conscious, he wouldn't lead in silent prayer! He was afraid of his shadow; as naive and inexperienced as you can imagine, with the worst case of hypochondriasis that I've ever seen. He was preoccupied with his *condition.* And he was miserable.

Clyde took the challenge and worked hard. He learned it was okay to have *feelings other than fear.* He learned that being angry was not a sin, and expressing it wasn't either. Early on in his therapy, saying "darn" in a *still small voice* was as close as he could get to emoting anger. That changed.

Equal in importance, Clyde learned he wouldn't implode if his meds were out of sight. The first big breakthrough was the day he came to a session without his medicine bag. He confessed it was outside in his car. Nonetheless, it was a big step for him just the same.

The man in the *imaginary protective bubble* unloaded a lot of emotional baggage. Instant improvement began when he discovered *change is a choice.*

Prior to therapy, Clyde's most courageous and daring life experience was archery! I'm not picking on archers. In fact, Martha and I used to shoot bows a little. It was during her first pregnancy (which about says it.) Archery is just not a daring sport that will pump up the adrenalin.

It's about as exciting as croquet.

After Clyde's intensive, with a brand new self-image under his belt, he vowed he was going home to change all that. And he did. Indeed, he did.

Several months later, Clyde wrote me that he was going to be in our area and wanted to come by for a visit. He wanted to tell me about his *new life,* and he wanted to take me for a ride while we talked. The ride was in his brand new fire engine red Mazda RX 7 with a stick shift.

Leaving the Center, he turned into the street burning rubber. He zipped around traffic, turned sharply, down-shifting like a teen with his first taste of power and speed.

Irregardless of being strapped in tightly, I was white-knuckled from holding on for dear life. Even though I was scared to death, I was chuckling. Is this really the bubble boy? The guy with three sets of meds?

Clyde told his post-therapy story. He had quit his job, moved out of his mother's house (much to her chagrin), and had relocated to another city. He had taken up ballroom dancing. For the first time in his life, he had gone out with several women. He had eliminated most of his medication. He had a *new life.*

Arriving safely back at the Center, I breathed a big sigh of relief. Clyde pulled out a pack of photographs.

"Don, these days, I'm not as interested in resisting temptation as I am finding it! Take a look at my latest passion," he explained as he handed me the photos.

My mouth dropped open as I saw the first picture. Clyde's first sky diving solo! All the photos were of him sky diving. One showed his mother on the ground waiting for him to land. I was surprised she hadn't croaked.

Looking at the photo of his first jump, I asked, "What thoughts and feelings were you having?"

Laughing, he said, "I knew you'd ask that! It wasn't very pretty but it was real. I felt like a caged bird that had just been released. Had never felt so totally in control of my own life. I wanted to scream to the top of my lungs, '____ you mother, and the horse you rode in on! ____ the doctors. ____ the world! Bubble boy is ready to fly.'"

Clyde, of course, did not say those things to any of those people, and rightly so. That's just what he *felt* like saying, and he had reached the place when he could share all his feelings without fear of being judged or criticized.

Clyde's mother, bless her heart, had done the best she knew how to do. Her worry over his health was understandable. But, her over-compensation meant the treatment had been more debilitating than the disease.

In a ten-hour seminar I lead, entitled "The Birthright of Every Child," one segment is called **Parents Don't Have a Chance**. This section is presented just before taking a break so I can smile at the people who tell me how relieved they are to hear these remarks. If the opportunity were hers, I think Clyde's mother would be one of them.

Parents really don't have (much of) a chance. Due to the fatal flaw in the human family, parents damage their children. Our best hope is to learn from the generation before us and at least pass on better material.

When our children were young, I often told them, "I know I'm doing some damaging things to you that you will have to deal with later. But I'm trying hard to pass on fresh neuroses rather than the same old stuff!" They didn't know what I was talking about, but I did. For sure,

I wasn't always successful, but I was trying.

One of the saddest things I witness is the trash that gets passed on down the line, generation to generation. By contrast, one of the most invigorating things I witness comes from working with those who determine to stop it. And they do. In so doing, the benefits of the evolutionary process continue to emerge.

Some of today's parenting is obviously atrocious. But in my view, parenting today is better than it's ever been. We know more about parenting than we're ever known, and a large segment of today's parents are doing a better job than any parents in the history of the world.

From my perspective, good therapy includes wading through your childhood history, not in order to blame your parents, but to discover and own the truth. We don't blame or chastise Clyde's mother. She did the best she could with the tools she had and what she understood. But she could have done better. And in order to learn from that, we can dissect what she did, learn from her mistakes, and do better. Clyde did.

Without in-depth therapy, Clyde would have parented the way he was parented. Consequently, another generation would have been riddled with intense anxiety and the fear of living. Thank God, he chose to change himself and the lives of the next generation. May his tribe increase. And may we all encourage today's parents to put their parents generation under the microscope, learn from their mistakes, and do better. Just makes sense to me.

(More on parenting in next chapter)

Chapter 16

What Do You Owe Your Parents?

> "Middle age is that time in life when the worries you have for your children and your parents are about the same."   Author

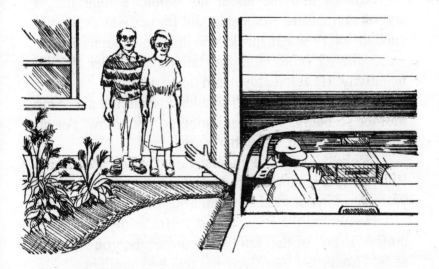

In the therapy room, it is common to hear people talk about **owing** their parents with such statements as:

"Well, she is my mother. At least I owe her a visit, now and then."

"After all, in spite of all our disagreements, he is my father, you know. I do owe him some respect."

"After all my parents did for me, I owe them more

than I can ever repay?"

"My mother never lets me forget how much I owe her for giving birth to me."

"My father believes that I will be indebted to him for the rest of my life."

The list goes on because our culture teaches that adult children **owe** their parents. Regardless, of whether or not the parent is cold, distant, or even abusive, adult children are taught that they **owe** their parents.

Roland told me about his mother's long list of constant criticisms. Nothing he did for her was ever good enough, long enough, quick enough, or ... enough. But he was quite uncomfortable just talking about her chronic negativity. He felt disloyal and disrespectful.

"I'm sorry," he said, "I shouldn't be talking about my mother so badly. She is my mother, you know. For all she's done for me, I owe her a great deal."

"Roland," I said, "I understand what you are saying. But you're a competent and capable adult man. Why do you tolerate your mother's ludicrous behavior?"

He quoted the Bible to me, "Honor thy father and mother is one of the Ten Commandments, you know? I should honor her more, and not talk bad about her."

"Yes, I know, " I said, (having heard that response at least a zillion times from those in therapy.) "I'm not wanting you to dump on your mother. I'm just wanting you to get some relief from your depression. Telling the unfiltered truth about your life, including your relationship with your mother, is the first step."

"Well, I don't know," he said. "I'm still hung up on that honoring your parents commandment."

Seeing how depressed he was, and how stuck he was on this biblical issue, I went to that verse for a little scriptural exegesis.

"Roland, it's not my job to change your belief system. What you believe is your business. My job is to point out to you the things that I believe are contributing to your depression. In order to do that, I'll have to challenge your assessment of that commandment. Are you okay with that?"

"I certainly want and need your help. So, I'm open to whatever you think I need to hear."

"Great. Roland, in my opinion, the interpretation of the commandment: *Honor thy father and mother...* has been grossly distorted and abused. This verse has been used as a mantra to lead us to believe that honoring parents means putting them on a pedestal, relating to them in reverence, taking whatever they dish out, *because* they are parents. Well, I must tell you that I take exception to that exposition."

Knowing how much he valued the Bible, I played my trump card.

"Roland, I studied Greek and Hebrew, and a better translation of *honor*, which comes from the Hebrew word *kavedh*, means **to value, to take seriously**. Honor is contrasted with *dishonor* which from the Hebrew means **to take lightly, to be frivolous, or indifferent.**"

Apparently, I sold it pretty well because he was quite impressed. He shouldn't have been. Let me explain.

While in seminary, I was terrible in Greek. I've often said, "I know a little Greek-- he weighs 120 lbs." I was worse in Hebrew. When I discovered Hebrew read right to left, and back to front, I knew I was in deep trouble. But, by then, the term was half over!

My Hebrew professor, Dr. J.J. Owens, was a language genius, and a wonderful man. Although language studies came easy for him, he had great empathy for those like myself who found language study (especially Hebrew) to be incredibly difficult. But the things I loved best about J.J. Owens were his warm smile and great sense of humor.

One day I said, "Dr. Owens, I'm so frustrated with Hebrew, I've considered cheating."

Lovingly known as Old Red Top, he replied, "Don, by the looks of your work, you don't know enough to cheat. I'll have to cheat for you." (Thank God, he did!)

However, in spite of my weak knowledge of Hebrew, Roland was quite impressed with my understanding of the Holy language, so I continued.

"Honoring your mother doesn't mean tolerating anything she dishes out. You'd be *honoring* her more by refusing to tolerate her criticisms any longer. In so doing, you would show that you **value** her, and are taking the relationship **seriously**. Tolerating her behavior is making you sick, and destroying your relationship with her. If you want to *honor* your mother, you must confront her."

He agreed that my exegesis was convincing, but his life-long indoctrination was too deep. Consequently, he continued to become depressed each time he visited with his mother, which wasn't often.

In Roland's mind, he *honored* his mother by not confronting her. So, he stayed away from her as much as possible. When he did visit, he *honored* her by tolerating her criticisms and rejections because, "...she is my mother, and I owe her that." (Is something screwed up about this picture, or what?!)

Okay, what **do** adult children owe their parents? Tolerance? Cards? Calls? Visits? Gifts? To take care of them? Provide lodging? Supplement income? Intervene for treatment? Force a nursing home? Is that what an adult child owes their parent for bringing them into the world, and raising them to adulthood?

I don't think so. These things should be done out of **desire** rather than duty. That's what we choose to do because we care, because of concern, because we love. But we don't owe our parents those things.

What then, do adult children owe their parents? **Nothing**. To me, parents owe children; adult children don't owe parents. Parents are obligated to children; adult children aren't obligated to their parents. Adult children are obligated to their own children, not their parents.

If an adult child wants to do, give, and provide all of the above things for their parents, that's great. But, in my view, they are not obligated. They do not owe a debt.

What I'm taking issue with is the concept of parental indebtedness. I am not proposing for adult children to neglect, snub, or mistreat their parents. Not at all. I'm challenging the idea that parents have an emotional, accounts receivable, ledger sheet that represents what their children OWE them because they are their parents.

What bothers me the most is the damage such thinking does to those relationships. And from the numerous stories I've heard, such attitudes produce substantial conflict.

Now I'm going to contradict myself and tell you what I believe adult children *do* owe their parents. For me, I've concluded my adult children owe me one thing, and one thing only. Namely, **to do a better job in personal development, partnering with their spouses, and parenting their children than I did.**

It is my greatest desire that my children do better than I did at being *persons, partners, and parents.* To learn from my record of successes and failures in personal growth, marriage, and family and build on it-- that's my only request. That would be a terrific payback for the efforts I made in parenting them, and partnering with their mother. And I hope my grandchildren do an even better job in personal development, partnering, and parenting. And on and on. Generation to generation.

If I'm fortunate enough to reach old age, I do not want my children tending to my needs out of obligation. If they *choose* to be caregivers for my old age needs, that's fine. However, they do not owe me anything. I just want my children to do a better job in relating to themselves, their spouses, and their children than I did. If they do that, I will consider their debt paid in full-- plus of course, repayment of the student loans!

Being better in these areas means giving them the freedom and encouragement to cut their own path, and pave their own road. Not doing it as I did it-- but better.

For most parents, giving freedom and encouragement to their adult children to run their own lives is a tough task. It was for me, as this story will attest.

Matt, our oldest child, was a freshman at the College of San Mateo (California), and living at home. One afternoon I was talking with him about something that had upset me. I proceeded to clean his clock over what he was doing or not doing that I thought needed adjustment. Can't remember the issue. Amazing, isn't it, about selective memory!

Finishing my exhortation, without knowing what I was getting into, I said, "Do you have anything to say?"

"Yes, I do," he said. "Dad, all my life, you've said by high school graduation time, you wanted me to make my own decisions, think for myself, be my own person. Repeatedly, you've told me to be independent and make my own life choices. Sounds good, Dad. But do you know what you really want? You want my choices to be in agreement with yours. You want me to be my own person, provided I'm like you want me to be. You want me to do all these things the way YOU want them done. Dad, you can't have it both ways."

To say he knocked the breath out of me is a gross understatement. Without answering, I excused myself and took a walk around the block. I knew he was right. Totally. All that talk I had done about being autonomous, independent, self-actualizing was based on my hidden agenda. Actually, I believed if he did those things, he would not yield to peer pressure, and would surely make the same choices that I would make-- being the All-knowing, All-wise, Miniature-Messiah that I was!

The most humbling part of that experience was realizing I was still capable of acting like I wore a Crown of Thorns. At that point in my life, I thought I had wised up enough to officially give up the messianic complex and permanently come down off the cross. But in part, that's what parenting does to you-- brings you down to earth, into the reality zone. Parenting, like few things I know, can take you off the throne and put you on your knees.

Back to my story. After a second time around the block, I returned with my tail between my legs, an apology on my lips, and a pledge from my heart. I promised not to tell him how to run his life anymore. I would give him advice *only* when he asked for it. I would offer my opinions on anything that related to his life, *only* as opinions. And I promised to work very hard in keeping the promise.

Fifteen years later, I believe he would tell you that I kept that promise. (Well, maybe once I broke the promise. Okay, twice. Okay, okay, three times!) And I'm pleased to give you the current status. Matt is my associate at *DFCC*. He is thirty-four, and a much better therapist than I was at that age. He is a better husband than I am, a better father than I am, and a better man than I am. I couldn't be prouder. He has already paid me far more than he owed with an added bonus-- a great sense of humor.

Last Father's Day, he gave me a card that read: *Dad, thanks to your lectures, I never change horses in the middle of a job worth doing; I know the squeaky wheel gets the worm; and I never count my chickens until I've walked a mile in their shoes.*

After a card like that, do you think I ought to make him doubly repay his student loans? Maybe I will!

Chapter 17

A San Francisco Treat

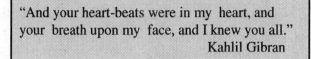

"And your heart-beats were in my heart, and your breath upon my face, and I knew you all."
Kahlil Gibran

"Betty," he said, "I've always wanted to walk across the Golden Gate Bridge. Let's take some wine and sour dough bread in a back pack and drive to the North Vista Point; then walk across and back."

"Sounds great to me, Burt," Betty said with enthusiasm. "Just say when."

"How about this afternoon? We could get there in time to watch the sunset while we're on the bridge."

"It's a date," affirmed Betty. "I'll pick up the goodies

and be ready when you get here."

With careful deliberation, Burt had set it up. As they reached mid-span of the Golden Gate Bridge, while overlooking San Francisco Bay to the East and the sun setting over the Pacific Ocean to the West, Burt O'Malley asked Betty Bakker to marry him. She said, "Yes," and as they say in South Georgia, they kissed several many times. Then they shared the wine and bread in what was certainly Holy Communion in perhaps its highest form.

As Burt and Betty ate from the same loaf, and drank from the same cup, surrounded by one of the most spectacular sights in the world, they knew that only God could have pulled off such an unlikely match up. Yes, this was Holy Communion, for sure.

Hold that beautiful romantic image in the corner of your mind while I rewind the tapes of these two lives and bring you up to speed.

Burt had been a mainline Protestant minister who moved to California from Pennsylvania for two distinct reasons: (1) he was coming for intensive therapy; (2) he was leaving behind a bag full of heartache and pain. He came to stay. Unfortunately, although he did not intend it, he brought his baggage with him.

For starters, the baggage Burt brought from back East to the far West included: (1)being burned out on the church; (2) the residue from a painful divorce; (3) and the lifetime frustration of being smothered by his mother.

To say Burt was an angry man is to undersell it as bad as calling the Grand Canyon a pothole. To say most of that anger was directed at everyone who qualified for the female gender is to be quite accurate. Like ships, churches have traditionally been issued the feminine pronoun *she*, which had added to his disdain for the Lord's organized body. One story will verify my point.

Burt said it was during the prelude of a Sunday morning worship service that he realized he was in deep trouble, and desperately needed some immediate help.

As the congregation sat in meditation and prayer, the final strains of the organ began to fade. It was now time for him to step to the lectern, and with a voice of reverence and comfort say, **"I was glad when they said unto me, let us go into the house of the Lord."**

Burt said he was overwhelmed with the urge to utter something quite different. Quite different, indeed. What he wanted to do was walk to the lectern and shout, **"It's b.s.! It's all b.s! Do you know that every last bit of this is b.s.?!"**

Fortunately, he quoted the Psalmist and finished the worship service. Then, he called the Bishop, resigned his position, and made an appointment for intensive therapy. That was the new beginning of his journey toward wholeness.

Let's push PAUSE for the Reverend Burt O'Malley, and rewind the tape for his wife to be, Betty Bakker.

For two successive Wednesday evenings, I had been the guest speaker at Betty's church, a vibrant body of believers in Daly City, California. It was a two-part series entitled, "The Condition of the Soil Determines the Fate of the Seed." In my presentations, I had talked about childhood experiences that affect our spirituality as adults, in the same way that the condition of the soil affects the planted seed.

Betty was impacted by these presentations. However, she was embarrassed for anyone to see her talking to me-- afraid they would think she needed therapy!

After the second meeting, she followed me to my car and asked for a business card. Shortly thereafter, she called the Burlingame Counseling Center to make her first appointment.

At the heart of Betty's problem was a huge *father wound.* While she was quite young, her parents had divorced. Mother was granted primary custody. Betty's father had been extremely negligent in maintaining a relationship with his daughter. She had numerous painful memories of sitting on the curb with her bag packed, waiting for a father who didn't show up.

Children have great sensory ability but very limited interpretative skill. Betty, therefore, interpreted her father's behavior to mean-- *he didn't like her, and didn't want to be with her.* To her, this meant-- *she was a bad little girl, was undesirable, and unlovable.*

Needless to say, as an adult, her self-image was very weak, and her self-confidence quite limited, especially regarding men. In turn, she expected to be rejected and discounted by men and had a hair-trigger in that area.

So, how did these two get together? Well, it wasn't easy! Both did individual therapy, working hard to heal their woundedness and to rewrite their life scripts.

After extensive individual work, I encouraged Betty to join my weekly therapy group. She had grown tremendously in self-esteem and self-assertiveness. She had confronted her father regarding the issues she had with him. For a time, he had even been in the same therapy group with her. (Now that's another story! Another story, indeed!) Betty had claimed her worth and had learned to stand her ground rather well. And she loved it.

No longer embarrassed about her need for therapy, she frequently introduced herself by saying, "Hi, I'm Betty, and I'm a neurotic!" Then she would add, "Don't let that bother you. It just means I had some painful childhood experiences that affected my life as an adult. Bet you're the same, huh?" (As a result of this boldness, she was responsible for numerous people getting into therapy.)

Back to Burt. Like many other men, his emotion of choice was anger and all emotions were channeled through that conduit. After emoting a lot of pain through his tear ducts, rather than clenched fists, his hostility had dissipated, a little. I thought he was ready for group therapy. He wasn't so sure. With much reluctance, he agreed to join the group, the one that included Betty Bakker.

Did you solve the *Wheel of Fortune* puzzle by saying, "Burt and Betty Push Each Other's Buttons?" If so, you win the Maytag washer and a year's supply of Tide. These two were so hostile toward each other, it was a small miracle they walked across the Golden Gate Bridge without either one of them jumping or pushing the other! Believe me, they pushed each other's buttons.

As a result, they took the next step in the therapeutic process:
(1) They learned to share feelings without over-emoting.
(2) They learned to be honest without being cruel.

(3) They learned that being real can be tempered with discretion.

Eventually, they began to go out for coffee after group; sometimes with the others, sometimes by themselves. (That particular group always told me that the *real group therapy* began after I went home.)

When relationships begin with honesty, openness, trust, and vulnerability, then emotional intimacy has a great foundation on which to build. Thus, the relationship between the Rev. Burt O'Malley and Betty Bakker grew, developed, and matured.

Six months after the storybook engagement on the Golden Gate Bridge, I conducted their wedding in Betty's church. Several group members attended. It was very special. Betty was beautiful, radiant, and confident. Burt was calm, smiled through the entire ceremony, and was not tempted even once to shout, "b.s.! It's all b.s.!"

Burt and Betty O'Malley have been married fourteen years, and now live in Klamath Falls, Oregon. They are enjoying life, each other, and adore their twelve-year-old son, Josh.

SELAH. AMEN.

Chapter 18

A Tale of Two Lives

> "Eternity is a place for broken things too broke to mend."
>
> John Masefield

Prologue: He was thirty-seven years old, single, and lived alone. On March 23, 1998, he wrote a final note, went into the barn, and ended his life. Thus, the last chapter of a seven-year horror story was written for Mike Reed. As the oldest son of my wife's sister, he was my nephew. At the family's request, I delivered the eulogy portion of the funeral.

Mike was the victim of a despicable mental illness, paranoid schizophrenia. His symptoms included: intense fears, sinister hallucinations, severe obsessions, and excruciating paranoia which eroded his joy of living, and finally took his life.

He is survived by his parents, Kay and Roy Reed; two brothers, Mark and David Reed; a sister, Tonya Reed Walters; a nephew, Dustin Reed; three nieces, Haylee Reed, Karlye Reed, Mackenzie Walters; grandparents, Doug and Mary Longmire Fowler, and a very special Uncle, John Houston.

All of Mike Reed's family are deeply dedicated to the process of helping victims of mental illness, and families who have experienced suicide. With their encouragement, as a tribute to this young man's life, and with the firm belief that "God is at work in all things to bring about something good"(even from this horrible tragedy), I have included the eulogy in this volume.

****

A Tale of The Two Lives of Mike Reed

"It was the best of times; it was the worst of times." Thus, Charles Dickens began his classic novel, <u>A Tale of Two Cities</u>.

Having known Mike Reed for his entire life, and having been a member of this family for nearly that long, it occurred to me that those words succinctly described the life and times of this young man and this family.

So, the title of this address is a paraphrase of Charles Dickens-- <u>A Tale of The Two Lives of Mike Reed</u>. I will divide my remarks into two parts: BEFORE his illness, which was the *real* Mike, and "was the best of times;" AFTER his illness, which was the *impaired* Mike, and "was the worst of times."

******

Part I: The Worst of Times

THOUGHTS ABOUT HIS ILLNESS. Although some subtle signs had been seen earlier, the full-blown, clearly visible symptoms of his impairment began about seven years ago when he was on a trip by himself to Greece. It was there that he had his first psychotic episode which means that his judgment, logic, and rationale were off-center. From then until now, there were good and bad days, rational and irrational times, normal and abnormal experiences, healthy and unhealthy behavior. But the unfiltered truth is-- these last few years have been more bad than good, and have been sheer hell for Mike and for his family. Let me explain.

Some infirmities, such as heart disease, strokes, and cancer, primarily attack and impair the body. Other diseases, such as Alzheimer's, dementia, and mental illness primarily attack and damage the mind. Mike had an illness that attacked and garbled his mind, distorted his perception and logic, and changed his personality.

Sometimes a physical illness will seize an individual who is strong, robust, and athletic, and turn them into a weak and frail shell of the person they once were.

Likewise with some mental illnesses. Sometimes a person whose nature is fun-loving, easy-going, and logical can become something completely different that scarcely resembles the person they once were. That was precisely the type of mental illness that crept into his life.

Mike's illness reminded me of the horrible disease that destroyed his grandfather nearly twenty-five years ago. Both illnesses lasted a long time. Both destroyed the person they once were; one's body, the other's mind. ALS (Lou Gehrig's disease) is a horribly debilitating illness of muscles, nerves, and the body. Paranoid schizophrenia is a horribly debilitating illness of reason, perception, and the mind. One took a life at age fifty-seven, the other at age thirty-seven.

Throughout both illnesses, family and friends did everything humanly possible to arrest and destroy the heinous culprits, with little success. Each of them lost, and we lost-- the battle, but not the war. Because the calling from God is not to be successful but faithful. In both cases, that victory was won with a slam dunk.

THOUGHTS ABOUT HIS DEATH. In my humble opinion: (1) Mike Reed did not intend to hurt his family and friends. (2) He was not expressing resentment at life, circumstances, or God. (3) He was not demonstrating hatred toward himself with this act of self-inflicted violence. (4) From my view, he was destroying a demonic disease that had tormented him for too long. He killed an illness that had snared him in a trap and would not let go. Even though his thinking (at the time) was distorted and irrational, that sinister sickness has now released him forever. Mike destroyed the tormentor.

The tendency for us all was to be upset and frustrated because he refused to seek help, and resisted taking his medication. But, we must understand *resistance* and *denial* are the predominant symptoms of the illness itself. In fact, that's the most diabolic aspect of this horrific malady. Paranoid schizophrenia overpowers it's victim by destroying reason and judgment, and convinces its prey: "There's nothing wrong with you. You're fine. Don't listen to them. You don't need help."

So, do not think that Mike's resistance to seeking help and refusal to take his medication was just being stubborn and irresponsible. It was *his illness* that was acting irresponsibly. It was *his illness* that was talking, feeling, and reacting in such an uncooperative manner. The core symptoms of this affliction makes treatment extremely difficult and terribly frustrating for the caregivers.

When most people have a physical ailment, they make some attempt to deal with it. However, the disorder that trapped this man convinced him that he was not ill, and did not need treatment. And no one could have convinced *his illness* otherwise. We could have convinced Mike, but the REAL Mike seldom "lived in there" anymore.

Neither Mike, nor we frail human beings, could match the tormentor that plagued him and overpowered him. And I hate that, I really hate that.

THOUGHTS FOR THE IMMEDIATE FAMILY. As we watched this drama unfold, all of us experienced intense sadness and resentment because it was so senseless. And everyone feels a certain amount of *natural* guilt because we were so helpless to stop it.

Such guilt is basically expressed in two forms of thinking and feeling: *I wish*, and *What if.*

"*I wish* I had done more and tried harder."

"*I wish* I had acted or reacted differently."

"*I wish* I had said more or said less."

"*What if* I had tried one more time?"

"What if I had prayed one more prayer?"

"What if I had gone earlier, or called sooner?"

This is a normal part of the grieving process, especially regarding suicide. But the truth of the matter is-- this family did all it knew to do, could do, were allowed to do. They prayed, and prayed, and prayed. They coaxed, pleaded, and begged. They had three interventions and were successful in forcing treatment through one of those confrontations. The results were still tragic. Those are the facts. Nonetheless, these facts will not eliminate our shame, guilt, and remorse about this horror.

So, the healthy thing to do is to allow ourselves to have those guilt thoughts and feelings, and then release them. The unhealthy and destructive thing would be to obsess, worry, and make ourselves sick over what we-- *did not cause, could not fix,* and *could not control.*

There's no value in endless talk or worry about what we should have done for this good man with this awful illness. Everyone who knew him and truly loved him did all (I said ALL), within their understanding and power to help. It was not enough. His efforts and our support failed; not from lack of trying, but from insufficient ability.

Someone very special died a few days ago. But the truth is, he lost his life, and we lost him a long time ago. And even as devastating as this tragedy is, perhaps every family member has experienced a slight sense of relief that this awful nightmare is finally over.

THOUGHTS FOR THE EXTENDED FAMILY & FRIENDS.

To talk with people who have experienced tragedy is always difficult. I've been asked countless times:

"What should I say?"

"How should I say it?"

"What is appropriate?"

"What is not appropriate?"

In our culture, when that tragedy includes mental illness and suicide, the difficulty factor increases ten-fold. Mental illness has always carried a stigma, and suicide has always been taboo. In turn, the awkwardness, discomfort, and uneasiness about *what to say*, and *how to say it* is even more uncomfortable, awkward, and uneasy.

So, to the extended family and friends, let me encourage you to put aside your discomfort, and talk with this family about this illness in the exact same manner you would any other illness that has tragically claimed the life of another victim.

Share your feelings with them and ask all your questions. In so doing, (1) they will be helped by telling you all about it; (2) you will benefit from hearing it; (3) and perhaps, just perhaps, God will use this tragedy to snatch someone from the jaws of despair.

Severe mental illness and thoughts of suicide are not really any different than any other life-threatening illness. Talking about it won't fix it, but it's a giant first step. And that could be a consoling memorial and legacy to this young man's life and death.

THOUGHTS ON THE HAUNTING QUESTIONS. Why does such a tragedy happen? How could a good family have such an awful experience? How could such a good boy and fine young man become so troubled and disturbed? Why would such a family-loving-man, do such a horrible thing to himself, his parents, and his family? And how in the world do we cope with this suffering?

I can't answer for you. But for me--the answer to these haunting questions is-- they are unanswerable. There's no rhyme nor reason for such atrocity and suffering. There are no soothing answers, no logical rationalizations, or explanations that make any sense.

In this human arena in which we live, life at its core is filled with ambiguity and ambivalence. We don't really know very much for sure. We have mixed feelings about almost everything. And that produces anxiety in us all. That's the way life is. And in the face of senseless tragedies, the only way I have found to *cope* with these unanswerables, is to consistently--

1. Celebrate life as a gift, but never a possession.
2. Stand in awe of the mystery, but never stop asking questions.
3. Live each day one day at a time, just doing the best you can.

******

Part II: The Best of Times
Who *was* the real Mike Reed?

He was a fine young man who loved the outdoors, loved to fish and hunt, loved to hear a coon dog howl, and loved being with family and friends.

Who was Mike Reed before he got sick?

He was a young man who loved old dogs and old people and spent a lot of time visiting with both, and talking to both. And did he ever love to talk! He would talk to a total stranger for hours on end, (a trait he acquired from his father.)

Roy once got a wrong number, long distance, phone call and talked for fifteen minutes before the other party knew they had the wrong number. Mike told me that story and thought it was hilarious because he knew he could have done the same thing.

Who was he before his illness?

He loved life and he loved to laugh. He could watch endless reruns of his favorite television programs. Could you guess what they were? *Hee Haw, Gomer Pyle,* and *Andy Griffith.*

As he put it, "Shoot, that's the only thing on television worth watching."

And he could wear you out with intricate details of each episode. The way he talked about Andy, Barney, Otis, Gomer, Goober, Howard, Floyd, and Ernest T. Bass, you'd think they were his personal friends who met daily down at Canale's store.

Who was the authentic Mike Reed?

He was loving, thoughtful, and generous. He enjoyed giving special gifts at Christmas, especially to the men-- knives, flashlights, a variety of novelties, or whatever else caught his fancy. The gifts were never wrapped. Always in a brown paper bag. As gifts were being opened, he'd go around the room handing out his presents and saying, "Yount-one-a-these?"

Who was Mike Reed in the best of times?

A person who loved to show you his newest gadgets and toys. He loved sharing his stuff with you. Example: In the mid-80's, he bought a Corvette from his youngest brother, David. He always told everybody "I got a great deal on the Vet." But he repeatedly told David, "You stuck me pretty bad on that deal." Whichever was the truth, he loved that car and loved showing it off. Martha, our children, and I were living in California at the time and were back here for a visit. He wanted to give me a demo ride in his car.

"Don," he said, "I want you to drive my Vet."

As I climbed under the wheel, he got in on the other side. I turned on Houston Levee Road and idled along until we rounded the curves just south of the Milton James place.

When I hit the straightaway, Mike said, "See if it'll run. Punch it." Well, I punched it. And it ran. I mean, it leaped. As we crossed the Wolf River Bridge, my first surprise was the number on the speedometer, which I will not divulge at this point. The second and even bigger surprise was the "blue light special," compliments of the Shelby County Sheriff's Dept.

Hitting the brakes, I pulled over, muttered under my breath something less than Sunday School talk, and said, "Well, what do we do now, Mike?"

He snickered that little trademark laugh and said, "What do you mean WE, you're driving."

Man, did he get some mileage out of that experience! Seeing his minister/uncle trying to talk his way out of a traffic ticket was something he never forgot. Nor would he let me forget it. I never will.

Who was he before his sickness?

As a kid, a teenager, and young adult he had a good heart. Because of that good heartedness, he's always been the subject of more funny family stories than anyone else.

Who was Mike Reed?

Well, he was opinionated, independent, and tenacious. (Tenacious is just a sweet word for stubborn.) Believe me, to say he got those traits naturally is a gross understatement. From Grandma Kilavos and Granddaddy Longmire, he got a double dip of being opinionated, independent, and tenacious. And we loved him for it.

Who was the real Mike Reed?

A young man whose life was much too brief. Actually, life is short for all, just shorter for some than others. But, indeed he crammed a lot of living into a short period of time. Thank God, death does not end the living of such a life. This fine man will live on forever-- not only in the great beyond, but forever on this earth through the memories he left behind.

That's something to celebrate by singing the hallelujah chorus, saying a prayer of thanksgiving, or reciting the requiem hymn from Holy Scripture:

"Nothing shall separate us from the love of Christ... not death, nor life, angels, principalities, or powers... not things present, nor things to come, not height, depth, nor any other thing in all creation, shall be able to separate us from the love of God, in Christ Jesus our Lord." (Paraphrase of Romans 8)

Who was Mike Reed in the best of times?

He was a Boy Scout. A good Scout. An Eagle Scout. Receiving his Eagle award in April of 1978, was one of the high points of his life. And rightly so.

The Scout Oath begins: "On my honor, I will do my best...." It goes on to pledge three things which then become the three fingers of the Scout Sign and the Scout Salute.

"To do my duty to God and my country, and to obey the Scout law;
To help other people at all times;
To keep myself physically strong, mentally awake, and morally straight."

I've always been impressed that the consistent thread that runs throughout the Scouting program is the emphasis on *doing your best*. Given his circumstances, I believe Mike Reed did the **best** he knew how, and the **best** he could, with the **best** he had.

The Scout Law has twelve points which read:
"A Scout is: trustworthy, loyal, helpful, friendly, courteous, kind, obedient, cheerful, thrifty, brave, clean, and reverent."

In the best of times, the REAL Mike Reed was all of those things. And for that we celebrate, give thanks, and salute him.

******

Epilogue: The response to the eulogy was shocking to me. I've never had such affirmation and appreciation from a funeral address. Calls, cards, and comments with words of approval came at a surprising rate (and continue as of this writing.)

All of this felt a little awkward, and actually made me feel a bit uncomfortable. Of course, I was delighted to know that my words were meaningful. But it felt strange to be getting such praise from something so tragic. Also, I couldn't quite understand why my address had ignited such applause. There was nothing extraordinary about my remarks. I offered no insightful answers, and gave no comforting solutions.

My delivery was at best, just average. In fact, I was incredibly relieved that I had been able to get through it without being overcome with emotion. Mike was a nephew with whom I had a close relationship, not a distant relative with whom I had little connection. So, for me, just getting through the eulogy with dignity and grace was the best I had hoped for.

Why then, was the response so overwhelming? I couldn't account for it. But as I continued to reflect on it, I remembered something that was said to me immediately following the service that explained the extraordinary compliments.

The funeral director told me personally, "I've been in this business for forty years and that's the first time I've ever heard the words *mental illness* and *suicide* spoken at a funeral. I'd also like you to know that's one of the best eulogies I've ever heard."

Bingo. It was the honesty that did it. I had used those off limits, secret-keeping words-- *mental illness* and *suicide*. Apparently, that honesty was very unusual, surprising, and emotionally relieving.

Strangely enough, as I prepared the eulogy, it never crossed my mind to whitewash the truth. To me, being asked to speak at the funeral meant they wanted me to tell Mike's story through my head and heart. Therefore, diluting the truth and avoiding using the words mental illness and suicide was not an option I could exercise.

As a boy, I grew up around both experiences. Two adults in my neighborhood committed suicide; and three members on the Doyle side of my family went through bouts with mental illness. In addition, a few years ago, one of my favorite cousins took his own life. I've never kept any of those experiences a secret. Nor have I viewed those tragedies any differently than if the victims had been plagued with a debilitating physical ailment such as cancer or heart disease.

Perhaps these personal experiences diffused any reservations I might have had about bringing the reality of Mike's death to a public forum. I'm not sure.

What I am sure of is-- the openness and honesty definitely impacted those who attended the funeral in ways I never dreamed of, and for that I am humbled.

Having encouraged those present to talk with the Reed family, and with each other, about these issues seemed to have rung their bells. For them, it was a huge relief to hear the truth without sidestepping around it. In turn, it prompted people (in a sense gave them permission) to think about their own families and their own secrets. And it spurred many to take a giant step toward their own healing.

In therapy circles it's common to hear, "Healing begins when the secret is out." That being the case, the tragic death of Mike Reed was the catalyst that started many people down the road to recovery. For that, we are all grateful.

******

Eternal Father,

We thank you for the good years of Mike Reed's life. We grieve, dear God, over his tragic death. And we trust and firmly believe that you grieve with us.

Our wounded hearts will be a long time healing. But that healing will be enhanced if we can see some signs that his death was not in vain. We loved the good parts of his life; we trust that you will bring about something good from his death.

Dear God, through your Spirit, empower this feeble attempt to tell his story. Prepare the ears that hear it, the eyes that see it, and the hearts that feel it, to make the changes in their own lives that you desire for them.

We claim, even now, the peace that you give us in knowing that lives have been changed, victims rescued, and families strengthened, through the memory of Mike Reed.

AMEN

Chapter 19

I Thought He Walked On Water

> "Then God made grandparents, and
> it was very good."   Charlie Shedd

For as long as I can remember, he was white headed. But then, my mother says the same. She was the last of his nine children. She says even in her earliest memories, her Pa's hair was solid white.

Asa Rhodes was not a big man, standing only about 5'6", when he straightened up. During his later years, arthritis, rheumatism, and gravity had rendered him even considerably shorter. But I thought he was a giant of a man. Still do.

Asa never went to school, at least not enough to speak of. He couldn't read or write. Made an X to sign his name. Probably was an embarrassment to him, but he never showed that it bothered him. Neither did it bother me, cause I thought he was a mighty wise man. Still do.

Asa never made much money. Didn't have indoor plumbing till the day he died. He didn't leave much to his heirs; about an acre of ground, a little house that was about to fall down, a few sticks of furniture, maybe a dozen handmade quilts, and a family Bible. My mother was given the Bible. She gave it to me. It's a treasure that I cherish. He never had money to speak of, nor possessions with monetary value. He had no prominence, prestige, or power, but I thought he walked on water. Still do.

My reasoning? My grandpa *mastered the art of living*. Like only a few people I've known, Asa Rhodes seemed to me to have real *peace of mind*. Maybe it was due to the great relationship he had with all of his children and their children. I never heard a single relative say a negative word about him. But his sweet spirit was not restricted to his own family. He loved all people, and they loved him. He loved life, and it showed.

It's amazing how many little things I can remember about the man-- the things he said, the way he walked, the way he talked, and the little mannerisms.

In his later years, he only had a couple of teeth. Don't know how he managed to eat. But he did. He wanted his coffee just about two degrees below boiling. He always drank the first two swallows from the saucer. He'd lean over, sip the coffee from the saucer, and then make a noise that reflected enjoyment and deep satisfaction, "Ahhhh. Lissie, that's mighty good coffee."

He wore Duckheads long before they were cool. His were the overalls model, which he called "overhauls." I remember him singing, "Duckhead overhauls wear like iron, wear like iron, wear like iron. Duckhead overhauls wear like iron, they're the best that money can buy." Then he would laugh.

I think he had three pairs of Duckheads. The everyday pair was nearly worn out. The better pair was worn when he was "going to town." The best pair always looked new. They were saved for church and special occasions; with a white shirt, of course. His three hats were rotated in the same manner.

Asa farmed all his life, raising cotton and corn. When I was five, I spent a week with him and tagged along while he worked in the fields with his cotton crop and late summer garden.

In a horse-drawn wagon, pulled by a team of horses named Major and Dan, we took the cotton to the gin. Wearing one of his old hats, I sat up on top of the cotton alongside Pa. A portion of the ride was on the highway. Old Dan had always been a little skitterish when a car would pass. Pa had him on the right-hand side and depended on old Major to hold steady in the middle.

Every time a car passed, Dan would jerk and whinny. Pa would laugh, crack the reins, call out to Major, and reassure me. I think it helped. But, I was still scared-- a little.

One day, Pa needed to plow the garden. He said he

needed me to ride Major, and make Old Dan work better. We were plowing right along, but Major seemed to be shirking on the job, maybe from being annoyed with me on his back.

In a reflex action with the plow lines, Pa popped Major on the rear. He bucked. I went flying off his back. Landed on the ground between the team. The oversized hat fell over my eyes. As I tried to get free, I kept bumping into horses legs, and I was crying. Pa felt so bad, he couldn't stop apologizing. As he hugged me and wiped my tears, I could see the fear in his eyes.

In his later years, he spent a lot of time *studying* in the front porch swing. That's what he called it. In today's lingo, we might call it meditating or processing. He called it *studying*.

When he was asked to make a decision on something, typically, he would postpone by saying, "I'll need to study about it."

When you greeted him with "How're you doing?" his answer was always the same: "Tolerable, just tolerable." Then he would chuckle.

The chickens were not penned up at Pa's. They wandered around in the yard, and in the flower beds where the cannas and elephant ears grew. Sometimes, they paraded around on the front porch, and frequently left their droppings, which Pa called "chicken puddin."

No way around it, periodically you would step in the chicken droppings. If you were barefooted, well, that just wasn't real cool.

One day, when I was around five or six, I stepped in a pile of fresh chicken manure. Being barefooted, it squished up between my toes. Running to the door, I yelled, "Help, Mother! I just stepped in chicken ___."

To put this in the proper context, let me digress for a moment. According to my mother, there were certain words that were known as *ugly words.* And I had just said one! At that age, I was old enough to *know* ugly words, but definitely not old enough to *say* one. I'm still not-- according to my mother.

Well, my mother, ever on duty to see that actions and language were acceptable, chided, "Oh hon, don't talk like that. That's ugly!"

Pa retorted, "Son, tell her it ain't ugly, just NASTY!" He roared with laughter. So did I. Thank God, so did my mother.

He was married twice. Fleatie Rogers, his first wife, and mother of all his children, died at age sixty. I was two years old. He married Melissa Johnson two years later. We called her "Ma Lis." My parents took them to the courthouse to get married. I was with them.

On the way back from the wedding, driving along a graveled country road, we jumped a little rise in the road. I was standing in the back on *the hump* holding on to the back of the front seat. The quick up and down motion prompted me to say, "I nearly peed in my pants." Yep, you guessed it. Another one of those ugly words.

My mother responded, "Oh hon, don't say that. That's ugly."

Pa to the rescue. "Zula, don't worry about it. I nearly did too!" And of course, he laughed. Ma Lis didn't laugh, at least not out loud. But I think she snickered a little.

Asa sure knew how to pick marriage partners. I don't remember Fleatie, but all the stories about her were incredibly positive. The one that impacted me the most involved a horrible tragedy.

During the flu epidemic of 1919, the whole family caught it. They were quarantined at home. Friends brought groceries and left them in the road. One of the daughters, Rethea, almost four, died of that awful illness. Fleatie got out of her own sick bed and prepared her daughter's little body for burial.

Fleatie birthed eleven children, including a stillborn, and buried a four-year-old. As an old friend from South Georgia would say, "Them was hard times." Yet, all the stories about Fleatie were positive and upbeat. They say she smiled a lot.

His second wife, Melissa Johnson, was a gem. Even

though she was an extremely modest and shy woman, she was very affectionate. And she loved to cook. The family's favorite dish was her fried pies-- apple and peach. No one knew when she made them, nor exactly how she did it, over that yellow and green woodburning stove.

One thing was sure. No matter when you came to visit-- morning, noon, or night, on any day of the year-- you could count on it, Ma Lis had fried pies. In the warmer drawer, of that yellow and green woodburning stove, was a stack of heavenly hash.

You didn't have to ask. She made it easy. When you gave her a hug, she'd whisper in your ear, "The pies are in the warmer." As I write this, I'm positive I can smell and taste them right now.

Back to Asa. I've never known a man more loved by his children. All five sons and four daughters stayed in touch with him on a regular basis. The consistent affection they expressed was truly remarkable. I could write for hours about Asa Rhodes. Someday, I will. But for now, I will stop with one final point that summarizes the man, his life, the peace of mind that he achieved, and how he impacted my life.

My fondest memory of Pa Rhodes was the way he said "Goodbye." From my earliest recollection, until the last time I saw him just three months before he died in the summer of 1967 when I was twenty-five, it was always the same. Without fail, at the end of every visit, his parting instruction never varied. "Son, just do your best."

The way he said it was not a command, a challenge, nor an edict. It was a simple, though elegant, reassurance about *finding the missing peace*, being contented with life, being in harmony with self, others, and God. "Son, just do your best."

Yes sir, I thought he walked on water. Still do.

******

As I've listened to people tell their stories, I continue to be amazed at the impact (both positive and negative) of grandparents. The self-esteem of a child who grows up in a hostile home environment is sometimes salvaged by a loving grandparent. Conversely, a child's self-esteem is often devastated by a harsh and hateful grandparent.

Everybody ought to have a grandparent like Asa Rhodes. Unfortunately, they don't. But everyone that does or did will never forget it. I won't.

My prayer is that I will pass on to my grandchildren just a little of what Pa Rhodes gave to me. I don't expect them to think I walked on water-- but hopefully they will think I did a pretty mean back stroke.

Chapter 20

Daddy's Girl Gets Married

"The most difficult experience for a father in endorsing his daughter's full womanhood is the day she gets married."   Author

The last chapter in this volume is a very personal family story. It differs from the previous stories in that it has a totally positive theme. The purpose of its inclusion is to show that even positive life experiences can produce feelings of loss, often require adjustments, and prompt changes in our lives.

*****

For me, it started in third grade. I'm talking about

public speaking. The poem I recited in the talent contest was entitled, "I Am A Fisherman." It went like this:

> I am a fisherman ho, ho, ho,
> Away to the creek I'll cheerily go.
> I am a fisherman hi, hi, hi,
> Fish by the dozen tonight you can buy.

I can't recall the next four lines, but I do remember that the "ho, ho, ho and hi, hi, hi" became "hey, hey, hey and hee, hee, hee." Hopefully, my public speaking improved after that. At least, the content.

During a career that has passed three decades, I've spoken several thousand times to a wide range of audiences. These experiences have included speaking before large and small groups; gatherings of old folks and young people. Some were occasions of celebration and inspiration; others were times of great sadness and desperation. The majority of these experiences were great fun. Some were very difficult-- particularly the funerals for family and friends.

However, I am ready to confess to one and all that one of the most difficult public speaking engagements of my career occurred June 3, 1995. That's the day my daughter got married. That's the day I escorted her down the aisle, gave her hand to the groom of her choice, and proceeded to conduct her wedding. Yes, I am convinced beyond a reasonable doubt, conducting my daughter's wedding ranks high on the list of difficult public speaking experiences of my life. And I truly believe that will be the case until I cross *the great divide*.

Leanne is our second child, born almost four years after Matt. She was born in Louisville, Kentucky, where

I was in graduate school at the time.

On the night before she was born, I was trying to finish a term paper that was due the next day. While I was typing away, Martha informed me that the labor pains were getting pretty strong. She thought we needed to head to the hospital. I persuaded her to let me finish the paper first. That transgression, I'm sure, has never been forgiven. Rightly so.

We arrived at the hospital at one o'clock in the morning. Mary Leanne didn't waste any time and made her way into this life at six o'clock. What exhilaration we felt to have a girl child to go with our boy child! From that day to the present, Leanne has always been the *apple of her daddy's eye.*

When she was nineteen, she gave me a treasurable Christmas present. It was a picture of the two of us with her head resting on my cheek and shoulder. Framed in brass, it was inscribed, "Daddy's Girl." I guess that about says it.

As a little girl, she frequently called me at my office. When I answered, in her slow and heavy Georgia accent, she would say, "Dad-e-e-e, this is Lea-a-a-n-n-e," (as if I wouldn't know unless she told me.)

For her twenty-first birthday, I took her on a three-day trip to New York. We had a super time doing the touristy things in Manhattan. Since both of us enjoy walking, we spent a good portion of the time on foot walking the soles off our shoes. It was August and New York was having a heat wave.

One afternoon, after we had been walking and sightseeing for several hours, I said to her, "Honey, we need to get something to drink, I'm afraid you're getting dehydrated."

A little while later, I said, "Are you sure you're drinking enough fluids?"

She began laughing uncontrollably.

"What? What's so funny?" I questioned.

"Dad," she said, "do you know how many times today you've asked me if I was getting enough fluids?!"

Reflecting on it, I realized I was still treating her like a child. She had been away at college for four years, but I was still relating to her like a kid who wouldn't know to drink enough fluids! Realizing the absurdity of it all, I started laughing and exaggerated the irrationality of my behavior.

"Yeah, I don't know how you've made it through the past four years without being dehydrated. I'll bet there are some days, while you're away at school, when you probably faint from lack of fluids. Yes sir, it's pretty lucky for you that I'm along on this trip, or you'd probably look like a dehydrated prune."

Thus, that trip was one more hurdle which I crossed in letting *Daddy's Girl* become a woman. The highest hurdle, however, was yet to come, which leads me back to the wedding.

It was a great honor to me that both Kelly and Leanne wanted me to perform the ceremony. But I was terrified that I couldn't do it without getting all blubbery, losing my voice in the jaws of emotional overload, and falling down in a puddle of tears! How's that for over dramatizing?

Yes, I had conducted Matt and Wende's wedding a

few years earlier. To be sure, that was emotionally difficult. And I had made it through their entire ceremony with repose and control. Until the very end, that is. When I got to the final pronouncement, my voice broke and my emotions were much more evident than I had wished.

No, I'm not bothered by people seeing my feelings or hearing me show emotions. But I don't want to make a fool of myself. Certainly don't want to be an embarrassment to my kids. As a matter of fact, to be an embarrassment to your children in public is probably one of parenthood's most undesirable experiences.

No, I don't think my show of emotion at Matt's wedding embarrassed my kids. But it was a near miss-- at least to me.

However, to conduct Leanne's wedding had two huge extra dimensions. Namely: (1) I was also going to escort her down the aisle; (2) she was *Daddy's Girl*!

Please don't misunderstand. It was not my desire for her to stay single. She was twenty-seven and ready to be married. Nor was I bothered by her choice of a husband. Kelly Duncan is a fine young man. He is an outstanding optometrist whom I deeply respect and love. I was totally comfortable with Kelly being Leanne's husband and my son-in-law-- even if he was a Dallas Cowboys fan, which brings up a slight diversion.

The night he talked to Martha and me about giving Leanne an engagement ring, I shocked him with my response.

"Kelly," I said, "you and Leanne will make a great pair. Your personalities can work together to build an outstanding marriage. And I believe you will. You love each other, and we love you both. But, to get my blessing, you'll have to meet two requirements."

Looking a bit like a deer caught in headlights, he asked weakly, "What are the requirements?"

"You'll have to agree to become a football fan of the Tennessee Volunteers and the San Francisco 49er's." (Kelly had been an outstanding college football player and was an ardent Cowboy supporter.)

Nervously, he said, "Could we negotiate on one of those requirements? Would one out of two be enough? It's no problem to become a loyal follower of the Big Orange. But, I don't believe I can ever pull for the Niners." (He still loves to tell that story.)

Meanwhile, back to my terror of being overly emotional trying to conduct Leanne's wedding. To put this in perspective, let me give you the big picture. I am a tender-hearted, nostalgic, melancholy, sentimental, emotion-filled, hopeless romantic. I get teary-eyed hearing the *National Anthem,* the *Navy Hymn,* and *Amazing Grace.*

The first time I saw a sunset in the Grand Canyon was a two-hankey scene. I go through at least a couple of tissues every time I watch Capt. Augustus McRae die in *Lonesome Dove.* When I hear Hank Williams sing *I'm So Lonesome I Could Cry,* I DO.

My throat hurts badly when Jack Shaefer has little Joey Starrett cry out, "Shane! Come back Shane. Shaaaane!" I'm still grieving the death of *Old Yeller.* Heck, I get goose bumps when Ole Smokey leads the Vols through the Power T in Knoxville on game day.

And I always have to blow my nose when John Ward cries out, "It's football time in Tennessee!"

Have I set the stage for you? Have I made myself clear? To walk my daughter down the aisle, place her hand on the arm of her groom, then walk up the steps and face a full-house congregation to perform the wedding of *Daddy's Girl* with dignity and grace, and not get emotional? A **large** order for this man, minister, and father of the bride. A very large order, indeed.

In planning for this experience, I wrote an original ceremony (which was much too long), and rehearsed it a gazillion times. To prepare myself emotionally, I wrote a poem to read at the rehearsal dinner. My reasoning was quite simple. If I could make it through reading my somewhat corney and syrupy poem during the *toasting,* at what would surely be an emotional rehearsal dinner, I could make it through the wedding. I went for it. And I made it without showing too much emotion. This is how it came out.

HERE'S TO LEANNE & KELLY

Over the years I've offered many a toast;
In the South, the North, and on the West coast.
Most have been pleasant, some quite a chore.
But I've never toasted a daughter getting married before.

I've toasted Matt's marriage, and his sweet wife so true;
Even toasted our beautiful, special grandson, too.
I've lifted a glass to young, old, for grads, newborns, and more.
But I've never toasted a daughter getting married before.

I've said "hear, hear" many times, to my 32-year bride,
With humor and laughter, and always with pride.
I've toasted birthdays at 20, and 30; twice for even four-score.
But I've never toasted a daughter getting married before.

I've done a high-five with Chad when he got his first deer.
And for that big trout in Montana, we saluted with a beer.
I've celebrated victories, in baseball, soccer, and football galore.
But I've never toasted a daughter getting married before.

So, for this new experience, and not knowing quite how to do it,
I'll just plod on through it, saying there's nothing to it, just do it!
To the Duncans, friends are us; Janyce, Dusty, Dallas, and Dave,
To the Doyle family, Kelly, is really quite a rave.

And, to Leanne & Kelly, I'll conduct your wedding and such,
Hopefully without fainting, or sobbing too much.
I'll walk you down the aisle, and say all the right things;
Let you say your vows and then exchange rings.

But, during the last part, when the minister says with pride,
To the groom with authority, "You may now kiss the bride."
Do not let it surprise you to hear me give the order,
"Kelly, if you meant what you said?!
   You may now kiss my daughter!"   6/2/95 dd

Well, I made it through the wedding with composure, and only a minimum of emotion. To be sure, it was an experience I shall forever cherish and never forget. I didn't embarrass my kids, nor myself.

Thanks be to God who gives us the victory through our Lord Jesus Christ. And thanks be to my physician who prescribed it and to Upjohn who made it-- a very effective and powerful tranquilizer!

Epilogue. Having thought about it at some length and depth, I've come to a tentative conclusion. I believe the most difficult experience for a father in endorsing his daughter's full womanhood is *the day she gets married.* And the most difficult experience for a mother in endorsing her daughter's full womanhood is *the day her daughter has a baby.*

Well, Martha and I have now been through both these experiences. Two years after her wedding, Leanne gave birth to a fine baby boy-- our second grandchild. A few days later, we had a family get-together to welcome the new arrival. I wrote him the following letter.

******

June 15, 1997

Austin Lee Duncan
1081 Woodgate Ext.
Humboldt, TN 38343

My dear little Austin,

What a treat it is to write this letter welcoming you into the world, and into our family. We're all here at your house on Father's Day to officially welcome you to our clan. Besides your parents, there are Uncle Matt, Aunt Wende, Uncle Chad, Cousin Brady, and of course Mama D is here, too. You are nine days old, and this is your very first party. Today is also another first-- it's your dad's first time to be honored on Father's Day. That's really special.

We've been waiting for you with eager anticipation. Apparently, you decided we had waited long enough because on Friday morning (June 6) you made it known that you were ready too, even though you were three weeks ahead of schedule. You weighed in at 7 lbs. 7 ½ oz. which is quite a big boy for someone arriving three weeks early.

They rolled your mom into the delivery room at 12:05 p.m. and at 1:05 p.m. they called us to come see her and you. What a sight that was! You were all wrapped up in a blanket and snuggled in your mom's arms. We all got to hold you -- your dad, Uncle Matt, Uncle Chad, and me. And of course, Mama D, who actually got in double time.

Guess what, they named you after your two grandaddies. Your grandaddy Duncan's middle name is Austin and my middle name is Lee. What an honor to be included in your name. Your mom also shares my middle name so I feel doubly blessed. Cousin Brady, (age three) is having trouble saying Austin Duncan. He calls you, "Ausum Dumplin" which actually may be quite accurate. We think you are pretty "awesome" and a sweet little "dumpling."

Austin, let me tell you about your parents, starting with your dad, Kelly. He's a fine man who comes from a good Oklahoma family with parents and brothers who love him a lot. Of course, they're going to love you the same way.

Your Grandpa Dave, Grandma Janyce, and Uncle Dallas drove all the way from Owasso to see you in the hospital the day after you were born. That really speaks well of the devotion and affection they're going to have for you and no doubt you will have for them.

Back to your dad. He's a hard worker and is doing really well in his career. He's calm, cool, and collected, and will be a good role model for you to emulate. He's really laid back and doesn't get upset very easily. However, over the next few years, you may test him in ways that he has never been tested! It kinda works that way. But, I'm sure he will be a good match for the challenge.

Your dad loves to hunt and fish. No doubt, he will introduce you to these great sports. Simply put, your dad's a great guy, and is going to be a fantastic father. I'm very proud to have him as my son-in-law and father to my grandson.

Now, let me tell you about your mom. She is strong-willed, determined, and tenacious which means she accomplishes or achieves whatever she sets her mind to. Uncle Matt and Uncle Chad say that means, "she always gets her way" which probably is at least partially true. But that's okay, her way is usually the right way.

Your mom is loyal, generous, and affectionate, and therefore, you are in for a treat as you will be the recipient of these great traits. Having her for a mom will be fun.

Quite simply, she has always been the apple of her daddy's eye. She was born at 6:00 a.m. in the morning. When the nurse told me we had a baby girl, I yelled out "yeee haww" which didn't impress the head nurse very much. Nonetheless, when thinking about your mom, I can honestly say that I have been yelling out "yeee haww" ever since. She's really special and is going to be a fabulous mother to you. She'll mother you in the same great manner that she was mothered. And believe me, Mama D is a role model who sets a very high standard for motherhood. But, there's no doubt that your mom will match it and even exceed it.

So, little guy, you are in good hands and you have already been uniquely blessed. You have a set of parents who love each other, and will expose you to a very healthy marriage. And they're going to see to it that you will grow up in a very healthy family. That's about as lucky as it gets. After that, everything else is just frosting on the cake.

Austin Lee Duncan, I know you've got a great life ahead of you, and I'm eager to watch you grow and develop. I'm

excited to be your grandpa who will watch from the sidelines
and cheer you on. Have a great journey.

    With much love,

    Papa Don

****

    Well, Daddy's Girl grew up, and got married (as of
this writing nearly three years ago.) Austin is almost one
and Leanne recently turned thirty. At nearly fifty-seven,
I'm well past middle-age. (How many people have you
known to live to 114!). But in spite of all that, Daddy's
Girl is still Daddy's Girl. This past Valentine's Day she
sent me a card that read:

To My First Valentine

No matter how grown up I get, no matter how far I go, no matter
who I meet, I'll never forget my first love, the first man in my life, my
very first and always valentine.

    Happy Valentine's Day,

Daddy's Girl

Epilogue

Riddle. *How many therapists does it take to change a light bulb?* **Answer**. *One. But the bulb has to really want to change.* Perhaps that's the common thread that runs through the fabric of the stories you have just read. *Common people can make uncommon choices that can revolutionize their lives **if they really want to change.***

Throughout this volume, you have been exposed to people who had the courage to change their minds. For some of them, results came quickly. For others, it required blood, sweat, and tears. In all cases, the courage to change their minds was the first and most important step followed by committing to make it happen.

The importance of repeating this seemingly obvious and simplistic truth is because it flies in the face of continuous contrary indoctrination. Such as:

"Well, that's just the way I am."

"You can't teach an old dog new tricks."

"A leopard can't change it's spots."

"Men are from Mars/Women are from Venus."

But all of these cliches are irrelevant, irresponsible, and erroneous. You can change. Give yourself the breath test. Put your finger under your nose and sniff. If you are still breathing, you can change. By choosing to change your mind, and then committing to do whatever is required to make it happen, you can change.

Several years ago, I was leading a parenting seminar for a church. The main subject was how children are damaged by faulty parenting, and how that goes on to effect their lives as adults. One segment was entitled "The Condition of the Soil Determines the Fate of the Seed."

Using the parable from Matthew 13 about *The Sower*

and the Seed, I presented, what I thought, was a fairly strong case in establishing my thesis. Namely: No matter how good the seed is, the potential for it taking root, sprouting, growing, and developing to fruition depends on the circumstances and surroundings in which it is planted. Just as the title says, "The Condition of the Soil Determines the Fate of the Seed."

The program had gone very well. During the exchange of ideas, it was obvious many of them had heard what I was trying to say, and had done some meaningful self-analysis. Even the question and answer period had been stimulating. In fact, it was during the Q and A segment, that the most memorable part of that evening took place. That's when a dignified, articulate, elderly gentlemen asked a question I will never forget.

"Doctor," he said, "You've given me some insight into some problems I've had all my life. But I do have a question. If the condition of the soil determines the fate of the seed, is it too late for me to change my *dirt*?"

The laughter subsided, and he sat down. With a smile on my face, and a lump in my throat, I replied, "No sir, it's not too late to change your dirt. If you'd like, I'd be honored to help you with the spade work."

My sincerest hope is that the stories you've just read will give credibility to the statement I made to that dear man. My prayer is that you too will find the courage to change your *dirt*.

The Going Sane Series

The *Going Sane Series* is a three-volume set. <u>Heroes of the Heart</u> was the first volume. <u>Change is a Choice</u> is Vol.II. Volume III will be released in the spring of 1999.

<u>Heroes</u> and <u>Change</u> are available in hardback, audio cassette, and workbook editions.

See order form on next page.

ORDER FORM

---

1. Telephone Orders: 1-877-467--2632 (Toll Free)

    737--6303 (Memphis Area)

2. Fax Orders: 901/751-4140

3. Mail Orders:

    Asa HOUSE Books

    P.O. Box 381604

    Memphis, TN 38183-1604

4. Please send____ copies of_____

5. Edition: ___Hardback

    ___Audio Cassette

    _____Workbook

6. Charges: $19.95 per copy, plus $3.00 for packing & postage. Tennessee residents only-- add 8.25% sales tax.

7. Name: _____

    Address: _____

    City, State, Zip:_____

    Phone: _____

8. Payment: __ Check__ Visa__ MasterCard

    Card number:_____

    Exp. Date: _____/_____

    Name as it appears on card_____

*D*oyle *F*amily *C*ounseling *C*enter
"Helping Others Heal Their Hurts"
*****

DFCC was founded in 1987 by Dr. Don Doyle, author of <u>Heroes of the Heart</u> and <u>Change is a Choice</u>. Matt Doyle, M.S. and Leanne Doyle Duncan, M.S. are the Center's two associate therapists.

DFCC is "A family conducting family therapy." Matt

and Leanne often work with the children and adolescents while Don works with the parents. This arrangement has produced some extraordinary results. (See testimonials.)

DFCC stands on the premise that the source of life's greatest pleasure or pain is based on the *relationship* one has with self, others, and God. Since this is our credo, we are firmly committed to the mission of assisting families, couples, and individuals resolve relational conflicts.

At DFCC, we never presume to tell anyone what they *should do, should not do, ought to feel, ought not to feel*, nor how they are *suppose to act*. However, if your life isn't fulfilling and satisfying, with kindness and compassion, we will give you our assessment of why that is true. Then, we'll offer our opinion of what you can do about it, if you choose, and then do our best to help you reach your goals.

From our perspective, achieving *spiritual and emotional growth through self-understanding* is the most effective means of healing relational conflicts. To accomplish this task, we utilize a variety of therapeutic methodologies. Our desire is to create a relaxing, disarming environment where:

> *trust* is built,
> *hope* is renewed,
> and *healing* takes place.

The therapy center and residential apartment are both designed and furnished to enhance this process.

Using *Relational Integration Therapy* in a traditional format or through the *IRIT* program, we're here to help relationships. If you need help in your personal life, marriage, or family, we'd be honored to assist you. The important thing to remember is-- *change is a choice*, and the choice is yours.

****

Intensive Relational Integration Therapy

Developed by Dr. Don Doyle, *Intensive Relational Integration Therapy* is based on the premise that personalities are: **formed**, **deformed**, **reform**ed, and **transformed** through relationships.

Therefore, the primary focus of *IRIT* is relationships-- past, present, and future. (1) We explore childhood issues, looking for damage that was done that is still affecting the present. (2) We look at the accumulation of adult experiences that is impacting current relationships. (3) And we develop a game plan to reduce the odds of repeating unhealthy behavior patterns.

IRIT will help you: (1) *Relive the past* so you can be finished with it; (2) *Rewrite the future* with realistic expectations; (3) *Rejoice in the gift of today* which is why it's called the present.

*The basic format is a one-week program that begins on Saturday and ends the following Saturday.

*Upon arrival, each client finds a packet of materials to be completed before the first session.

*Beginning on Monday morning, we do six non-stop hours each day, for a total of thirty hours.

*Daily homework includes reading, journaling, watching videos, exercising, rest and relaxation.

*At the end of the week, a three-month follow-up plan is prepared which is tailored to each individual or couple. Usually six to nine pages long, a portion of the last session is used going over the after-care proposals.

The concentrated format offers ample time to focus on *causes* rather than *symptoms*. This often includes reliving and releasing the hurts, hates, and horrors from past experiences. Sometimes it means discharging the psychic baggage from carrying around painful secrets.

Healing begins when the secret is revealed, which includes feelings that have been suppressed. Frequently, people expose these *secrets* in the first session; maximizing the healing process.

Many hurting people do *IRIT* work by themselves and resolve life-long problems such as: depression, panic attacks, eating disorders, sexual dysfunction, and assorted addictions. Others spend the week working jointly with a daughter, son, sibling, parent, or spouse. Couples with dysfunctional, long-term marriages suffering from deep-seated problems often transform their relationship.

IRIT is for individuals, couples, parents along with their adult children, and families who are ready for change. *IRIT* is about the four R's:

    *Recovery from emotional turmoil;

    *Retreat for spiritual contemplation;

    *Respite from daily stress;

    *Redirection for the next phase of your life.

If you're ready for some changes in your life, maybe you need to consider *IRIT*. If you're dissatisfied with what you're currently doing to bring about those changes, maybe it's time to consider *IRIT*.

Working in this format, many people have had life-changing experiences. Since 1987, due to the reputation and success of the program, clients from twenty-five states and five foreign countries have come to DFCC for *IRIT*.

Maybe it's time to make a very important decision in your life and call DFCC for an appointment. After doing an intensive with us, if you're not completely satisfied with the results, *we'll gladly refund your misery!*

<u>Traditional Therapy</u>

In addition to the concentrated intensive program, we also work in the more traditional format. For families, couples, and individuals who are within driving distance of DFCC, we see them on a weekly or periodic basis.

With the exception of our work with children, all sessions are two hours in length. Using two-hour sessions for more than twenty years, we get better results from one, two-hour session than two, one-hour sessions. Our clients enthusiastically testify in support of this claim.

****

<u>Seminars, Conferences, and Workshops</u>

The DFCC staff speaks to churches, schools, civic clubs, counseling centers, businesses, and corporations, on a variety of appropriate group meeting topics. Such as:

"The Birthright of Every Child"
"Boosting Your Child's Self-Esteem"
"A Survival Kit for Parents with Teens"
"Living With an ADHD Child"
"Learning to Like the One You Love"
"Building Lasting Relationships"
"Dealing with Addictions"
"Peer Counseling Workshop"
"Growth Group Leadership Training"
"Stress Management Training"

****

<u>Corporate Consultations</u>

DFCC provides a consultation service to businesses and corporations. The program is called *Positive Life Management Training* and consists of spending a minimum of one week at your facilities evaluating the interpersonal aspects of your enterprise. Using personal interviews and questionnaires to gather data, we put together a follow-up plan to help make your operation more professional, proficient, productive, and profitable.

******

<u>A</u>dolescent <u>S</u>elf-<u>M</u>anagement <u>T</u>herapy

Some teens need traditional treatment. Many do not. DFCC offers a new approach to adolescent problems. Employing a variety of techniques to empower teens to make positive changes, we help adolescents learn to change their behavior through our *Positive Self Management* program.

Utilizing their own motivation and ability to make positive choices, this approach offers help to those experiencing behavior problems. Through *PSM* training, teens learn coping skills necessary to handle: (1)daily stressors; (2) promiscuity; (3) eating disorders; (4) anger control; (5) insubordination; (6) drug and alcohol abuse.

Most teens who are in trouble possess the power to change their lives. With the tools provided through our *PSM* program, that power can be actualized. As a result, their attitudes change, their performance improves, and their self-esteem soars.

****

If you'd like your name or someone you know placed on DFCC's mailing list, please make sure we have the correct addresses.

For more information regarding DFCC's programs, services, fees, scheduling, insurance coverage, or free phone consultation regarding your issues and concerns, call or write: **DFCC   901/757-2347**
110 Timber Creek Drive
Memphis, TN 38018